LIVING FOR THE WEEKEND:
A Woman's Cry For Hope

*"Empowering Women to Creep Past The Pain
and Leap Into a Glorious Future"*

Dr. Robin Elliott

Copyright © 2016 by Dr. Robin Elliott

LIVING FOR THE WEEKEND: A WOMAN'S CRY FOR HOPE
"Empowering Women to Creep Past The Pain and Leap Into a Glorious Future"
by Dr. Robin Elliott

Printed in the United States of America.

Cover Design by Leighann Thomas ~ AestheticLeigh Designed LLC~Washington DC Metropolitan Area

ISBN 9781498481250

All rights reserved solely by the author. The author guarantees all contents are original and do not infringe upon the legal rights of any other person or work. No part of this book may be reproduced in any form without the permission of the author. The views expressed in this book are not necessarily those of the publisher.

Unless otherwise indicated, Scripture quotations taken from the Holy Bible, New International Version (NIV). Copyright © 1973, 1978, 1984, 2011 by Biblica, Inc.™. Used by permission. All rights reserved.

Scripture quotations taken from the New King James Version (NKJV). Copyright © 1982 by Thomas Nelson, Inc. Used by permission. All rights reserved.

Scripture quotations taken from the Holy Bible, New Living Translation (NLT). Copyright ©1996, 2004, 2007 by Tyndale House Foundation. Used by permission of Tyndale House Publishers, Inc.

This book contains stories in which the author has changed the names of some people in order to protect their privacy.

www.xulonpress.com

I dedicate *Living for the Weekend: A Woman's Cry for Hope* to my family who holds a very special place in my heart. Although there were times when it seemed like everything was coming at me all at once, you encouraged me to share with the world, the powerful message of "HOPE" that the Lord gave me to give to women. In spite of all the disappointment and pain I endured in the midst of encouraging my fellow sisters to *think* their way into a new dimension, with your support and kind words, I did it.

To my friends, both near and far who challenged me to lead without fear, and to love without limits, thank you for believing in my calling to a nation of women who are searching for someone who knows their struggles and who's willing to lead them to their destiny, without being judgmental. You were truly a blessing to me, as I unselfishly poured into their lives, even though trouble was knocking at my own front door.

Finally, to those with whom I worship, I appreciate your continued prayers and compelling words of encouragement while traveling through this thought-provoking journey for the sole purpose of edifying the Lord. I am truly grateful.

~ACKNOWLEDGEMENTS~

P.K. Bernard once said, "A man without a vision is a man without a future. A man without a future will always return to his past." First and foremost, I give honor to my Lord and Savior, Jesus Christ, for entrusting me with His boundless vision for my life. Vision, is a very powerful motivator, which establishes a platform for pursuing one's purpose. In one of his most uplifting messages, Bishop T.D. Jakes, stated that, "Living on purpose is to become aware that we were *all* created to serve some specific function in life." This statement alone proves that vision is paramount. Moreover, Pastor Rick Warren believes that a purpose driven life creates the premise for which we *all* exist. Although these pastors are among the most brilliant men in the world, and their widely accepted views appear to be as good as gold, if we fail to unravel our purpose, we abort our destiny. If we abort the destiny, we cancel the destination.

For years, I tried my best to suppress the vision God has for me, which is to empower women all over the world to "*creep* past the pain and *leap* into a glorious future." Needless to say, that after witnessing the deterioration of my innocent sisters' lives, I could no longer just sit on the sidelines watching them suffer at the hands of a malicious, cold-blooded coward, who was determined to wipe them out. Sadly, that is exactly what happens when we refuse to get involved. We take on the role of the innocent, self-righteous bystander, instead of standing by those who need us most. Boy, do we have it twisted.

After years and years of contemplating, whether or not, I was unequivocally prepared to take on such an awesome challenge, I finally put my fears to rest. I stepped out of my comfort zone and leaped into the lives of countless petrified women who spent hours upon hours pushing the panic button. The bond between us was so extraordinary that there was no doubt that I had discovered my true calling.

It is an honor to lead my sisters into a new dimension while they blossom into remarkable women of courage and purpose. Sometimes, we just need the right person to help turn our discombobulated lives around. Although it took a lot out of me to go at it alone, I would like for my family, friends, and acquaintances to be the first to know that, thanks to them, I am now operating in my divine assignment.

Mind you, being a courageous and purposeful leader comes with a hefty price. However, I embrace the challenge. I know I will have to stand tall in the midst of my own troubles, as I lay the groundwork for other women to triumph over their hurdles, but this is where my faith kicks in. I intend

~Acknowledgements~

to work tirelessly to help pull another sister up out of the trenches, brush her off, and send her on her merry way. It is my prayer that one day she will do the same and the domino effect will continue for a lifetime. Subsequently, there will be an army of strong, self-sufficient women, who are capable of standing up on their own two feet when the odds are against them. After all, isn't that what it's all about?

Moving forward, I would like to thank all of the women (whose names are too numerous to list) that encouraged me to write this book. You believed in me when others doubted. Some criticized and said it would never happen. Thank goodness I did not entertain their negativity nor did I think twice about who said it. My message to them was that these days, effective leaders don't necessarily have to be the ones who stand up in front of a crowd, or those who yell very loud. It just takes those of us who are dedicated to a greater cause.

A huge thank you also goes out to those individuals who knew my struggles and did not judge me, but rather, embraced my frailties by accepting me when I was at my worst. Thank you for believing with me; my assignment to lead women has become more evident than ever. Without your prayers and support, this journey, would have definitely been a lonely one.

Finally, thank you, thank you, thank you to my wonderful and talented niece, Leighann Thomas, owner of AestheticLeigh Designed LLC, for her stellar creativity in designing my book cover, as well as, her remarkable editorial insight, which has added a "touch of class" to the pages of this book. It is because of her professionalism and countless hours of burning the midnight oil that many of you will have an opportunity to discover what is on the inside. LeeLee, your amazing talents in graphic designing and commentary have definitely paid off. You are a jewel.

~TABLE OF CONTENTS~

Introduction xiii
A Special Note of Encouragement xxi

Chapter One~ When Pain Takes You on a Different Journey 25
How to put your painful circumstances on the back burner and leave and leave them there

Chapter Two~ Overcoming the Trials of Fear and Rejection 49
How fear and rejection can cause you to stop short of your dreams

Chapter Three~ Giants do Fall 73
How to slay the "giants" in your life

Chapter Four~ You Gotta Believe 93
How believing against all odds automatically declares you a winner

Chapter Five~ What to do When You're Feeling Hopeless 111
How doing the unexpected can actually change your life for good

**Chapter Six~ The Twenty-Four Hour
Woman Syndrome**..................**129**
Why it's okay to say "no" and mean it

**Chapter Seven~ Women and the
Woes of Life** **153**
*What happens when we allow our feelings
to get in the way*

**Chapter Eight~ Oh, How Sweet it is:
Recovering from Divorce and Defame** **185**
How to avoid being bitter after divorce: forgive

**Chapter Nine~ Look no Further:
He's the One.**......................**213**
How not to settle for the wrong guy

**Chapter Ten~ Faithful, Frugal, and
Fabulous.**.........................**229**
*How not to be broke, busted, and disgusted
before and during retirement*

**Chapter Eleven~ Now that You Are on Top:
What's Next?** **265**
*What happens with most of us when we
reach the pinnacle of success*

Conclusion........................**275**

~INTRODUCTION~

What will *you* do when you have fallen out of love with yourself and the hellacious storms of life have led you to believe that there is really nothing left? Will you slip back into a mode of unconsciousness that is doomed to drive you insane? Or, will you finally make up your mind to stop playing the preposterous blame game? Ladies, I dare you to be completely honest with yourself and stop blaming your frailties on everybody else. When you finally realize that you have no one else to blame, you *will not* have to worry about popularity, fortune, or fame.

Unfortunately, at some point and time in our shattered lives, we must face the inevitable. Some things are bound to go wrong. Just when we think we have it all together, something else pops up, that lets us know how warped our thinking really is. Those radical twists and turns our lives suddenly take often lead to life-altering circumstances that are simultaneously overpowering and oppressive. However, without an eminent resolution, our troubles are sure to alter the trajectory of our lives. In fact, the low blows that easily trigger our meltdowns and bad memories keep us awake at night with one eye open and the bedroom door bolted shut. Not only are we afraid to fall asleep and dream, satanic powers and demonic forces, overwhelm us with what we have to face when the clock strikes twelve, another day of pure agony and hell.

For some of us, the problems that catch us by surprise can actually cause the tiny little muscles in our eyelids to twitch, and our stomachs to rumble, as a result of being ill-prepared. Unfortunately, as our lives began to unravel, fear tramples over us like a herd of wounded elephants, escaping the gunfire of the skilled hunter. Once the elephants are unjustly stripped of their most treasured resource, their tusks, the hunter is satisfied at knowing that his job has been fulfilled, thus the hunt is finally over when the helpless elephant is brutally killed.

Regrettably, this is how some of us, unintentionally fall prey to an enemy that has an unflinching desire to destroy our lives. We often find ourselves ensnared in the same deadly booby trap, as the bamboozled elephants, when our vision is blurred. Cloudy vision causes us not to *see* or *think* clearly, so our purpose for living is butchered as a result. Therefore, we end up looking down the barrel of the enemy's weapon without a plan in sight. Just as the elephants' tusks are a valuable commodity to the seasoned hunter, the heartless enemy seeks to rob us of our most prized possessions, even if it means sabotaging our lives. I can almost guarantee that some of us will end up just like the poor elephants if we chose not to be wise.

As author of this self-help book, I felt compelled to write *Living for the Weekend: A Woman's Cry for*

~Introduction~

Hope for the purpose of empowering women to take charge of our precious lives, while breaking free of the bondage that has incarcerated our sometimes crazy and mixed-up minds. When we are hurting inside, no matter how hard we try, it is extremely difficult letting go of those idiotic thoughts of retaliation. This is one of the main reasons why we blame those persons who have had a hand in hitting us where it hurts, instead of owning up to the part we played in allowing ourselves to fall prey to their wicked little schemes that always seem to have a deadly chokehold on us. Subsequently, it is nearly impossible to move past the bitterness in order for us to get better.

Living for the Weekend: A Woman's Cry for Hope paves the way for all women to understand that we are certainly not alone when facing the repulsive storms of life. These aggravating circumstances have a very sneaky way of grabbing our undivided attention when we least expect it. Whether we like it or not, our problems are notorious for developing into massive tornadoes with destructive outcomes. Likewise, some of our troubles resemble electrifying whirlwinds that can potentially evolve into violent hurricanes with strong gusting winds and vibrant bolts of lightning. Disturbingly, we always find ourselves scrambling for cover when we are accidently caught off guard.

Incidentally, the unanticipated hardships *we* often face as women remind me of the tear-jerking scene from the movie, *The Perfect Storm*. It can easily be surmised that the fishermen's lives were in mortal danger when they were taken by surprise on the water. For the most part, many of our unexpected surprises are sometimes a double whammy and a bit much for us to handle alone. Could this be a strong indication that all *hope* is gone? Dear God, please don't let it be so.

Somehow, we have unconsciously allowed those raging storms to rock our boats for too long. Now it is time for us to start riding the majestically moving waves of destiny and pick up the tiny little pieces of our shattered lives. Are you ready to sail through the rough, murky waters of uncertainty, in hopes of discovering your purpose? Climb aboard. The friendly captain is anxiously waiting to take you on a spine-tingling adventure guaranteed to help rid those unyielding cobwebs out of your mind. Hold on tight. You are in for the ride of your life.

Living for the Weekend: A Woman's Cry for Hope speaks victory into the lives of hurting women whose promising futures were on the brink of destruction when they lost themselves in the midst of losing hope. Could something like this happen to someone like you or me? You bet it can. It happens to more women than you think. Most of us are incredibly good at hiding it though, so we stroll around town with masks painted on our faces as thick as the skin on a rhino's back.

This powerful, life-changing book, offers a plan of action for women that is sure to set us on the right track. It provides an array of wholesome strategies and useful tips on the joy of bouncing back. "Bouncing back from what?" you might ask. My response would be, "Bouncing back from the unsettling "woes" of life; the troubling situations

~Introduction~

that often curb our appetites." Most of these undesirable predicaments have a tendency of hanging around for a lifetime. However, I believe this time we have definitely found the cure.

Referenced among eleven chapters, are amazing strategies and alternative solutions, devised specifically for helping women unclutter our minds while living victoriously. Each chapter will take you on a remarkable journey through the life of a woman whose senseless suffering seemed endless. She could not get herself together to save her life. The problems she encountered along the way ranged from emotional abuse to financial ruin and everything in between. In spite of the despicable treatment from those she trusted, her unwavering relationship with the Lord gave her the guts to fight for survival, vowing to come out alive. I hope you will be able to identify with her external challenges as you discover how she overcame her trials, despite the tiresome toils she faced and the ridiculous ridicule that seemed impossible for her to erase.

These pragmatic explanations are referenced with women in mind, specifically, those of us who are on a serious mission to regain control of our lives. We no longer desire living in the dark shadows of ruthlessness nor do we aspire to remain destitute. It is now time for us to snatch our lives back. Are you ready for this long awaited journey? This time we mean business.

If you or someone you know can benefit from the spirit-filled messages that are waiting for activation in your lives; you have the right book in your hand. *Living for the Weekend: A Woman's*

Cry for Hope is for *you*, seriously. It touches the hearts and minds of women who are recovering from the scars and bruises of divorce, low self-esteem, insecurity, and more importantly financial ruin. These staggering issues can be debilitating if we do nothing to reverse the tumultuous side effects that come alone with them. This book is also for women who are suffering from co-dependency and educational and career setbacks. Oh yeah, we cannot forget about those of us who are victims of chronic depression stemming from a broken heart and broken promises.

By the same token, this thought-provoking publication, reaches out to women who are facing an "identity crisis" and have given up on life. Their dreams have been cast aside like filthy rags once used for washing away the muddy debris from an old rusty dusty beaten up car. When we toss them aside, they are useless and good for nothing. I am sure *you* do not want your dreams lying dormant inside of you, do you? I did not think so. Now, I believe you have finally gotten the picture. So, whatever you do, please do not allow anyone to kill the dream inside of you. In the words of Paul Valery, a French poet and philosopher, "The best way to make your dreams come true is to wake up."

As you are reading this inspirational publication, it is my prayer that you will conjure up enough nerves and do as I did. Go ahead; take that critical and life-changing leap of faith that you have been desperately dreaming of taking. Although I was scared to death of the uncertainty and backlash, that may have come about as a result, I stepped

~Introduction~

out on faith and kept on strolling. Eventually, my strolling turned into prancing and leaping. Before long, I was sprinting towards the finish line waving the baton in my hand. Perhaps Oprah Winfrey, philanthropist, CEO, and entrepreneur, said it best, "The biggest adventure you can take is to live the life of your dreams." What's holding you back from getting your life on track? Could it be those newly found relationships? Or, are you afraid of what others may say or think about you? If you answered "yes" to either question, you are not alone. I was too, so there you have it.

Thank God, that I came to my senses "in the nick of time" or I would have certainly vanished in the Sea of Self-Pity. Yes, there is such a thing. However, I was determined not to allow my unanticipated struggles to ruin my life forever, so I vowed to face my failures one by one. As the days grew longer, my fragile body became stronger; now I am no longer the same. I made up my mind that I would make it this time. I was tired of playing those silly, old, conniving little games.

Unlike most women who fear the unknown, I set out to do something about my creepy jitters that took me out of my comfort zone. Ultimately, I was yearning for a place of pure serenity. Now I can say, "I am happy being the woman that God meant for me to be." After months and months of searching for answers in all the wrong places, I realized that it was time for me to stand up and dry those bittersweet tears that I wasted for so many years. I also learned to face the challenges that were sure to come my way if I did not want my failures to be an instant replay.

Instead of feeling sorry for myself, which was the easy way out, I took a leap of faith determined not to doubt. This time around I was led by the Lord, so I prayed day and night to stay on one accord. He is an awesome and faithful friend to everyone I know. This is why deep down inside I *really* love Him so. Without Him in my life, I would surely fail, but I did not want that to happen since I was already catching hell.

Finally, from one sister to another, it behooves us to "*creep* past the pain and *leap* into a glorious future" even if the crutches of life are yanked right out from underneath both arms, and the fiberglass cast that holds our bodies in place to heal has somehow turned to scraps of steel. Do what others said you'll *never* be able to do. Then, when it is all said and done, you'll be a better you. Leap, my sister, and the net *shall* appear. Do it right now instead of waiting another year. I leave you with these exquisite words of wisdom:

> *"Start by doing what's necessary; then do what's possible; and suddenly you are doing the impossible." Francis of Assisi*

A SPECIAL NOTE OF ENCOURAGEMENT

As you're thumbing through the pages of the book, you'll notice that I've incorporated three incredibly user-friendly tools that will encourage you to *think*: *Question of the Day, Affirmations,* and a *Goal Setting Exercise* designed with you in mind. Dr. Cindy Trimm, a world-renowned life strategist once said, "You can think your way through just about anything." Well, as a certified professional coach, I wholeheartedly agree, but there *is* a slight problem. Sometimes, we are in need of a tool specifically designed to pick our brains in order for that to happen.

These valuable tools, at the end of each chapter will help you to wrap your brain around a variety of captivating questions, while exploring the greatness of your mind through pen and pencil. When answering each question, you will realize that not only will you be encouraged to *think*, but you will also be equipped to take action by using your mind instead of your mouth to fight back.

I have found in my coaching experiences that it is rather easy at times to coach someone else through their personal issues, but when the tables turn and our own issues are at stake, who will be there for us? Jotting down possible answers to various scenarios will have a profound effect on our lives when there is no one else around to help us settle down. You will be thrilled in knowing that the solution to your problems is right there at your fingertips.

It is my desire to motivate you to evaluate the inspirational, yet perky, picker-uppers I chose as daily affirmations. Affirmations are in place for emotional support that keeps us going, when in fact, we really want to quit. I'm pretty sure somewhere in your travels you've vowed to change your life for the better after hearing such effectual words, so why stop now? What an awesome revelation we get when experiencing the power of words spoken over our lives, even if we have to say them to ourselves in order to believe it.

My sister, please use these tools wisely. They can be a blessing in disguise when problems arise. Keep them by your bedside at night so when trouble comes along you will not have to fight. The affirmations that you vow to keep will sustain your life from week to week. These wonderful tools will most certainly come in handy, and if you use them correctly, your life will be dandy. Blessings!

~Reflections to Remember~

When Pain Takes You on a Different Journey

People who experience pain often fail to realize that without it, many of their ideas, visions, and creations would never be birth.

Many of us see pain as an obstacle, when in fact it should be viewed as an opportunity for moving in another direction.

When we're caught off guard by life's unexpected surprises, one of the best things we can do to circumvent the pain is to realize our potential for turning our lives around.

~CHAPTER ONE~

When Pain Takes You on a Different Journey

How to put your painful circumstances on the back burner and leave and leave them there

There are times in our lives when we think, "I am not going to make it. All hell has broken loose, or if somebody doesn't help me now, I am going to S-C-R-E-A-M." You may have even reflected on what would have happened if only you had known then, what you know now. Sounds familiar, doesn't it? Well, if any of these irrefutable thoughts have crossed your mind lately, you are certainly not alone.

Some women have walked through countless adversities during their lifetime. However, many have vowed to become stronger and wiser, while others like me, had almost completely given up on life. "Not her," they said. "YES ME," I screamed violently, while pacing up and down the haunted hallways of my home, frantically searching for a quick fix. "NO, OH HELL NO," I yelled at the thought of *that* happening to me again.

Anticipating the worst, I burst into tears and began sobbing like a newborn baby. In the twinkle of an eye, my unusually clam temperament suddenly exploded into sheer madness. "YOU HAVE GOT TO BE KIDDING ME," I hooped and hollered hysterically, while madly kicking and stomping on the antique furnishings nearby. "I DIDN'T DO ANYTHING TO DESERVE THIS," I affirmed, as I scurried throughout the house ranting and raving like a ruthless mad woman seeking revenge with my hair standing straight up on top of my head. Rummaging through the house for clues, my eyes grew larger than coconuts, while frisking every piece of furniture, and ensuring that nothing was overlooked as a dead giveaway. "COULD THERE BE SOMEONE ELSE?" I wept uncontrollably, while attempting to destroy everything in sight that dreadful and daunting night.

I can recall plotting to break and shatter the fine crystal china and gold stemmed glassware so eloquently displayed on top of the cherry wood buffet to erase my pain, but something just would not let me go there. What good would that have done anyway? The senseless thought of destroying priceless valuables would have only caused me more pain. I certainly did not need that nor did I have the strength for cleaning up the mess afterwards.

Everywhere I went trouble seemed to have been right there on the spot. It almost caused me to throw a hissy fit without thinking about the unfavorable impact my selfish reactions would later provoke. I felt like a raging bulldog prying its way out of a wooden cage, when flashbacks reminding me of the same scenario that I thought was finally buried, suddenly resurrected. Out of frustration, silly thoughts of wrecking the entire house lingered in my mind, as if that would help to alleviate my fears. Now that I think about it, that type of malicious intent would have been totally out of character for me.

While desperately trying to put the pieces of my shattered life back together, the words from an old cliché that my mother spoke of some time ago quickly came to mind. I figured there must be some truth to it; "If you think something is going on; then most likely it is." Mom was referring to a woman's intuition. I heard others say that women are born with it. The majority of the time we are on point when thoughts suddenly float in and out of our mind that seems to be giving us a warning. They come from either a prior experience or an inclination that something is about to happen, that requires action. However, sometimes we try to balance our natural inclination with what we know to be true. Initially, we are somewhat apprehensive about our hunches, therefore, we quickly dismiss them. Later on, we are in awe when we discover that we were right all along. But, is it too late?

Afraid to even imagine the trauma of reliving my past; my heart fluttered in fear. "Could this be my plight again?" I wondered, as a hopeless sensation of rejection lodged and lingered in my mind. After all, the alarming thought of someone else taking our place is every woman's worst nightmare, especially if this is the second time around.

We all have had foolish dreams of living a fairytale life where everything is prim and proper, unique and unmasked, and prosperity is a promise. However, while thinking about the path that my life had taken, I instantly broke out into a cold sweat, as tiny speckles of warm water sprouted from the pores of my grim and glowering face. At the same time, my mind was intensely searching for a way of escaping this horrific and hair-raising juncture in my life. To my demise, there was nowhere to run and no place to hide. Once again, the unnerving lifestyle I tried so hard to steer clear of was staring me right back in the face. This time, I was determined not to let it get the best of me.

"Could this be my destiny to live this life alone?" I squealed, while falling down on my knees to pray. With both hands gently folded across my damaged and distressed heart, I gasped and gagged for words of comfort. At this point, I slowly tilted my head towards the sky, while closing my weary and watery eyes. Just as I opened my mouth to speak, my chapped lips trembled, and my bony knees shook so hard that the large oval-shaped, animal print rug I was kneeling on almost slid right out from under me. Moreover, an unusually sharp pain in my spine sent sparks flying throughout my entire body. It created dismal and delusional thoughts of my once impeccable lifestyle slowly slipping away.

Shortly afterwards, my head began thumping and throbbing so hard that it rocked the bed in the exact spot where I rested my head in prayer. Right then, my heart started pumping and pounding at about a hundred miles per hour. It felt like at any given moment it would jump straight out of my chest and land on the floor right in front of me. Startled by this unexpected occurrence, I leaped to my feet, grabbing hold of the wooly bedspread that gave the room an inviting appearance. Unintentionally, I pulled the spread clean off the bed, while tightly clinching down on its ridges to prevent me from falling backwards and possibly splitting my head wide open on the corner of the razor sharp dresser. WOW! What a frightening experience that was. For a moment, I thought I was having a heart attack or something.

As I breathlessly imagined how my life would really end, out of nowhere, a small, still voice quietly whispered, "I AM WITH YOU; EVEN UNTIL THE END." Those soothing words of comfort and a boost of reassurance were just what I needed during that deplorable time. Remember, I was battling to prove my innocence and worthiness to anyone who would listen. Realizing that my life had taken a turn for the worst, I grudgingly crawled into bed and tightly squeezed my tear-stained pillow that was already wet from a cold sweat. I desperately tried to decipher what went wrong, recalling that dismal and appalling night that nearly change my life forever, but my mind kept reverting back to the promises he'd made.

As time went on, I vividly recalled the high-pitched ringtone of the cordless telephone lying sideways on the hand-carved nightstand next to my king-size bed. "Another sleepless night," I murmured and moaned, as my tired and lethargic body tossed and turned. For some odd reason, I just could not fall asleep, though I felt drowsy and sluggish after a long day's work. Moreover, cloudy visions of confusion and chaos drifted in and out of my head while I stared at the uniquely arranged antique pictures hanging freely from the freshly painted walls. Squirming like a worm, I eventually shifted my frazzled body from one side of the enormous bed to the other, in hopes of getting a good night's rest.

As I tried lying motionless, I could not help but wonder who had the nerve to call my house after midnight, as suspicion and speculation aroused my curiosity. Since it was way past my bedtime, I'd already spoken with family and friends, so I knew they were snuggled tightly in bed and probably snoring by now. Suddenly, my mind became weary, as the night grew long, cold, and eerie, while contemplating the grueling circumstances that were bound to come my way.

Glaring at the unknown number, I hesitantly whispered, "Hello," anticipating an apologetic or remorseful reply. However, as I waited patiently not a single word was uttered by the person on the other end. "H-E-L-L-O," "H-E-L-L-O." "WHO IS THIS?" I asked, maybe once or twice, although it seemed like the brief moments of silence lasted for eternity. Without warning, a deafening dial tone sounded loudly in my ear. Stunned by the caller's insensitivity, I listened intensely, with a scowling and scrounge look on my face while waiting for the phone to ring again. Of course, I waited in vain. It never did.

Before long, I was seething and sighing in rage while my ears burned like fire. My disgruntled face turned as red as the skin on a Cameo apple when I abruptly slammed the telephone back down on the hook, which caused the mouthpiece to split in half and the cord to disconnect from the receiver. "DEAR GOD, PLEASE WAKE ME UP FROM THIS NIGHTMARE," I insisted, hoping and trusting that this was just another bad dream.

Reluctantly, I glanced out of the corner of my eye and immediately the stillness of the night overpowered me. You could say that I was as helpless as a lamb as my entire body froze in place. "LORD, PLEASE NO, NOT THAT AGAIN," I wailed, as my numb and lifeless body lie stretched out across the bed. In desperation, I suspiciously ran my shivery sweaty hands across the other side of the bed and carefully pulled back the neatly tucked covers, only to discover that my gut feelings were now a reality.

As I sat spiritless and afraid to move, those same insightful words from that old cliché popped into my head a second time, as though they were giving me a warning, "If you think something is going on; then most likely it is." I was too dumbfounded to believe that these same ingenious words were probably true, but this time, I did not have a sensible plan to help me make it through.

Shamefully, I had to admit that hopelessness and heartbreak had overshadowed any signs of HOPE that the future held for me. I was on the brink of breaking down and giving up, just like many women do when we run into something unexpected. "Could it really be . . ." I stuttered, inching from the bed to the floor with a crazed look on my face. Then, while snooping through the spooky hallways, I was startled by an unusually loud noise that appeared to be coming from the room upstairs. "I wonder should I head in that direction," I mumbled under my breath, hoping that would satisfy my curiosity.

Cautiously observing everything in sight, I darted in and out of the rooms exploring all nooks and crannies before dashing up the flight of stairs with high hopes of embracing a warm and welcoming face. The closer I got to the door, the louder the joyful noise became. In anticipation of a quick peck on the cheek or an intimate kiss on the lips, I flung the door wide open at the exact time the jubilant crowd yelled, "S-U-R-P-R-I-S-E." What a low blow that was when I discovered the blissful sound was actually coming from a grand celebration that was taking place at one of my neighbors' houses down the street. "WHAT ABOUT ME?" I asked myself, as I nearly fainted in grief.

Disappointingly, I stumbled back down the stairs and started my search all over again, just in case I mistakenly overlooked the prize possession that I'd hoped to find. Once again, I found myself alone, afraid to move, afraid to explore, afraid of *life*.

While agonizing over my afflictions and catastrophic misfortunes, my stomach flipped upside down. I felt as though I had been stabbed with a jagged sword and my guts ripped out. "DEAR GOD, W-H-Y ME?" I asked in an inquisitive tone of voice, as I dropped to my knees again, gasping for a breath of fresh air. Pleading for an explanation, my frail body moved lifelessly across the cherry stained hardwood floor, and peeped around the corner into the family room for a safe place to hide from my fears. Clinging to my favorite chair, I limped from one side of the large room to the other, expecting to find serenity to help me get through this mid-life crisis. Instead, there was no peace to be found.

"LORD PLEASE HELP ME," I begged and pleaded until my voice became hoarse and my throat raw. With everything going on at once, I felt as though my future was chained and shackled with relentless regrets. My motivation for living had quickly vanished into a vapor of never ending smog. Although my purpose for living had been raped by endless pain, disappointments, and deceit, I just knew that somehow I would one day get back up on my feet.

After regaining my composure and giving myself a real Suze Orman "smack down" I dried the stream of salty tears from my bloodshot baggy eyes and deliriously gazed at the twelve-foot high ceiling, in misery. In a blustering voice, I cried out, "LORD . . . YOU SAID." Before I could even finish my sentence, a peaceful voice softly answered, "BE STILL MY CHILD." "How in the world am I supposed to be still with all of this confusion and turmoil going on?" I mumbled agitatedly, without realizing who I was talking to. Of course, I had to be obedient if I wanted to prevail. On the other hand, I was thinking, "Why was I going through so much hell?"

From past experiences, there was no doubt that my ex-friends were just waiting for me to crumble, and though I had a stroke of bad luck, I was strong-willed and serious about staying respectful and humble. Lost for words, and distracted by my crazy misfortunes, I could not help but to wonder when will this saga ever end. THANK GOD ALMIGHTY, I finally realized that life can be lonely and harsh without a *true* friend.

Just as I turned to head back to my room that same angelic voice surprised me and said, "I WILL NEVER LEAVE YOU NOR FORSAKE YOU." Those encouraging words of comfort truly helped to calm my fears, and it felt so good just knowing that someone GREAT and MIGHTY had my back. Right then, I knew without a shadow of doubt that I was on the right track, regardless of what others may have said about my life. If you want to make it in this cruel in which we live, sometimes it takes letting go of all you've worked so hard for in order to gain what the Lord has in store for us. Most times, it completely blows our minds.

What a shocker, right? This was not supposed to happen to an intelligent, successful, and "prissy" girl like me. After all, I was primed for success and well on my way. Shaking my head in disbelief, I grumbled in a muffled voice, "You never know what life has in store for you." At the end of the day, I too, had suffered the realities of a broken heart, just like most women. However, from this point forward it was up to me to sink or swim. I chose to put on a life jacket.

I can truly relate to most, if not all of the growing pains that women have experienced, throughout their lives. Not long ago my life was in shambles. Yes, mine. My faith had been shattered and my heart trampled and crushed. Like most women who suffered the frailties of life, my desire to live was a thing of the past. The dread of disappointment suppressed and paralyzed all of my dreams, visions, and ideas, plus, I was still wounded over the tragic death of my best friend, my darling mother, who had passed away from cancer.

Before I could barely catch my breath from that tragedy, the marriage, that I meticulously pampered and eloquently prayed for crumbled and collapsed. To add salt to the wound, I was falsely accused of cheating; the number one thing that would destroy even the most exemplary marital relationships. To me, this type of adulterous behavior was utterly despicable and totally disgusting. It would certainly *not* be tolerated by me at all. Blaming me for something he did was his sneaky way of covering up for his own wrong doings. Ladies, you know how that goes.

As the relationship worsened and eventually ended in divorce, undesirable feelings of shame and humiliation stayed on my mind. However, I refused to be distracted and blown away by the malicious actions of others who tried to suppress my success. I intentionally ignored the lies and slanderous remarks while trying to find my way, but it sure wasn't easy. Isn't it funny though how the accuser is usually the one who commits the crime?

A few months later, the well-established educational business that I birthed and maintained, folded. The tear-jerking pain *that* caused almost knocked the breath out of me again. I was mainly concerned about how was I going to make it if I was suddenly jobless, financially strapped, and alone at this stage of my life. Being in a place like this can send you into hysterics when your life makes a drastic turn for the worst. I bet most women would have this same type of uneasiness if all of a sudden their means of support was suddenly exhausted without warning. In spite of it all, I did my best to remain courageously strong, as my sister Sandy and I, grudgingly loaded tons of books and scholastic materials into the trunk of my car on the final day the business would be in operation. This time, it took everything in me to keep from freaking out and acting like a fool, as we cried our eyes out together through the entire move.

If the truth be told my life was all botched up. You would have thought by now I would have lost my mind. When friends offered their condolences to help me get through that shameful situation that hovered over my life, I refused their acts of kindness and pretended to have everything under control, but who was I fooling? I did this in order to avoid the embarrassment and degradation that was sure to circulate all around town. My life had instantly become an open book. There was no way that I could have kept it hush-hush. No matter how hard I tried, I could not phantom why things were going the way they were, since I'd always gone out of my way to do good to others. Everyone knew I would give my last dime, but how could I ever tell other women about the goodness of the Lord when my own life was a mess? Furthermore, how could I tell anyone how I almost failed every single one of those grueling tests?

As Sandy and I loaded the final box of items and remorsefully closed the trunk, out of the clear blue sky, a low-pitched voice softly said, "THIS IS NOT ABOUT YOU, MY CHILD." "How much more of this am I going to have to take?" I yelled so loudly that it felt like I was going to explode. Somehow, as I struggled and continued to pray for relief, I was able to reposition myself and landed right back on my feet. Those were some hard pills to swallow and for a minute, I thought I was choking to death on them. Honestly, I thought I wasn't going to make it. BUT, I SURVIVED. YES, I AM A SURVIVOR AND I DIDN'T EVEN HAVE TO FAKE IT.

Although looking from the outside in most would surmise that my life had been showered with fortune and fame. It appeared as though I had it all together, a mighty woman of God, an active community leader with a supportive family, and a school administrator. Working tirelessly with very few hours of sleep afforded me the opportunity to become a college professor and CEO of my own tutorial company for children and adults. I am very proud to announce that my tutoring business also won the Onyx Award for the Small Educational

Business of the Year in the state where I resided at the time. Oh yeah, I forgot to mention that I was also a former local beauty queen.

Sadly, the many accolades and accomplishments were not enough to ease my afflictions. I still felt crippled and depleted by the drama that was going on even though I was minding my own business. My personality was never a reflection of the kind of person who frequently visited neighbors or entertained hearsay through the grapevine; though I must admit it was quite tempting for me to do so at times. On a normal day, my usual routine included going to work, preparing dinner, and spending quality time at home or church with my family. As you can see, there wasn't time left in the day to do much of anything else. This is why I could not believe that I was catching so much hell.

Although I tried very hard living a life that was purposeful, productive, and would empower women to "reach for the sky" scandalous lies, incessant deceit, and boundless blame constantly poured from the mouths of those who vowed to love and protect me. Contrary to what was said, those same people turned their backs on me when I needed them most. I just could not understand their reasoning behind treating me as though I was a piece of nothing. "Was it true love or was I just an object of their desire?" I wondered, as I sat quietly meditating on how I was going to mend my broken heart.

Afraid of what the answers might have been, I shrugged my shoulders and lowered my head in despair, while praying that my suspicions were erroneous. So many times, I found myself hallucinating and daydreaming about how I wanted to live my life, but regrettably, my dreams had only panned out to be an illusion of another senseless nightmare. Unfortunately, alienation and rejection had become my closest friends, while darkness seemed to have found an eternal resting place in my heart. During those dark and gloomy days, I felt so low, as though I was the dirt underneath the belly of a pregnant ant. To me, that was as low as it gets. Once again, I refused to quit.

As if that wasn't enough, so-called friends would whisper and chuckle as soon as I scooted pass them on the way to my seat at one of my favorite places to eat. It was no secret that they were gossiping about the distasteful rumors of my downfalls which resurfaced all over town. Yes, I was "the talk of the town" as they would say, but in a degrading way. With my ears cocked forward and my bushy brows raised, I tried eavesdropping on their private conversations, only to discover that my hunch was on point. "They are laughing at me," I whimpered in a faint voice, clenching my fist in anger and grinding my teeth. My initial reaction was to retaliate and to go berserk by turning over tables and chairs and breaking tall stemmed wine glasses throughout the place. I even thought about jumping in their faces and using some of those inappropriate four-letter words that would certainly burn their ears to a crisp. However, I quickly remembered that, "two wrongs don't make a right."

Disturbingly, those who hated me were able to find humor on the premise that I almost had a nervous breakdown. Again, I had the upper hand because those rumors were absurd and certainly a farce. Holding back the tears and gently clamping down on my lips, I slowly picked up the white linen napkin from the beautifully decorated table and gingerly wiped my teary eyes, pretending not to care. Realistically, I could not stop thinking about the fact that people can be so cruel when "the shoe is on the other foot." However, since I was in it to win it, there was no turning back now. I was preparing for the fight of my life. Not the type of knock down drag out dirty fighting that you would expect from a mad woman, but a spiritual warfare was brewing. I was being led by the chief priest; the Lord God Almighty. Who do you think would win this battle?

Others sitting nearby had the audacity to giggle and point their fingers at me, as I darted in and out of the mischievous crowd, while leaving the unpleasant scene at the noisy restaurant. My adversaries would not leave me alone. They continued taunting and antagonizing me just for the fun of it. Would you believe I could not enjoy the seafood entrée that I ordered every time I dined at this popular little spot? I was so distraught and overwhelmed that I didn't want to face my foes to defend myself. It was evident that I needed every ounce of strength left in me to make it home and eventually to make it to the weekend. In my mind, if I could last two more days until the weekend, I could pull myself together and think things through after enduring such traumatizing and grueling experiences, which had already taken a real toll on my life.

To me, the weekend represented a safe haven, a place where I could find tranquility and peace. Tuning the world out and inviting the Lord in was what I looked forward to by the end of the week. On the weekends, I could kick back, relax, and put my troubles behind me, while searching for new ways to contend with my life. Also on the weekends, I loved spending quality time in prayer, focusing on my priorities, and discovering hidden talents that I never knew existed. Behind closed doors, I cherished the peacefulness that the weekend would bring. All I wanted to do on the weekend was to take a deep breath, calm my fears, and put my feet up. I knew exactly how I would spend my time once the weekend came; I just had to make it there.

The weekends also meant freedom. I was free from all of the hustle and bustle that prevented me from excelling in my career or moving forward with my life. Exhausted and practically worn out, my heart was set on the weekends because I could clear my mind of the clutter and the hoopla that seemed to follow me home from work every day. Finally, on the weekends, I often enjoyed the ambiance of a soothing candle-lit bubble bath and a tall, cold, glass of apple cider, while reading an interesting novel or listening to my favorite musical artist. Most of all, it felt so good not having to answer to anyone, nor explain anything that was going on in my life to anyone. That was the "icing on the cake."

Conversely, others also treasure the weekend after withstanding the demands of a laborious workweek, but in a much different way. Their plans for the weekend included socializing with friends and colleagues, "letting their hair down," and "living it up." For some, the weekend was a time to eat, drink, and be merry. The weekend had also become a place of comfort and rest for those who looked forward to it as well. However, while they relished their significant others, I also cherished spending time alone with my significant other, my Lord and Savior. Although I was living for the weekend, a glimpse of my life would have definitely revealed a picture perfect depiction of a woman desperately searching for HOPE.

As life went on, almost daily, I encountered those who consistently tried to orchestrate and manipulate my every move. Though they anticipated the worst, I continued striving for the best. "Give it all you've got" had suddenly become my motto for life. Some even took time to meticulously demonstrate how they would sabotage and shatter my dreams. Isn't it a shame how some people try to put their foot on your neck when you're down. However, they soon discovered that I wasn't about to be defeated.

My enemies heard of my mishaps and wanted to keep me down in the dumps. They even cheered and rejoiced as though they were celebrating a milestone in their own lives when they found out that I had dissolved my business and left town.

You would have thought they struck it rich or won the lottery by their actions. They enjoyed rejoicing at the thought of my demise. My adversaries wanted me to fail and fizzle away as though I never existed, so they conspired against me too. I was betrayed and demoralized by my confidants to boot. At the time, I could not stand to look at some of them. They had also proven to be two-faced backstabbers who were looking for a way to break me down, but the Lord was not about to let *that* happen.

For months, my critics declared and decreed that I would never recover from those terrifying episodes of almost losing everything, so they continued masterminding my faults and turning their noses up at me. I was even silly enough to think that I had lost everything I struggled so hard to get. At the time, the only sure thing that I could really rely on was the Lord. I knew He would *never* fail me. Furthermore, my life was not defined by stuff, which could be easily replaced by the one who enabled me to acquire it from the start. Thank goodness for *that*.

As time went on, some of my so-called friends still pegged me as being a "pushover." The rationale behind their silly thinking was based on my refusal to embrace their childish plans for retaliation. In other words, they wanted me to beat the heck out of those who were stirring up trouble. Subsequently, that would be something else for people to talk about; but I was too smart for that. In retrospect, they were the ones causing the problems. Several of my buddies were fierce and furious because they surmised that I was too scared to stand up for myself. Realistically, I did not have to. I knew the Lord would fight for me. He clearly said in His word that He would fight my battles if I trusted in Him. This time, I had to use His word as my weapon of defense.

While my life continued down that dark and lonely path, somehow I was able to find the strength to preserver by reciting one of my favorite scriptures from Philippians 4:13, *"I can do all things through Christ who strengthens me"* (NKJV). The reassurance that I had the strength to conquer the "giants" in my life was solely from the Lord, which emphatically solidified my faith in Him. Since David killed Goliath with the help of the Lord, I could definitely slay the "giants' in my life with His help. He was everything I needed.

In essence, there will be times when we all go through unwarranted and crushing circumstances that we wish we could close our eyes to and they will magically disappear. Don't you wish we could wave a shiny little golden wand in front of our faces or from side to side and all of our troubles will be over? Wouldn't that be nice? All of our problems would instantaneously vanish overnight.

In order for us to withstand any test or trial, we must be able to endure the aches and pains that come along with being victorious. Who doesn't want to win? Living victoriously is part of our DNA. It's the ups and downs, that we're afraid of. We must get our emotions in check and stop being afraid of everything. Isn't it ironic that we run from the very thing that will ultimately thrust us into

When Pain Takes You on a Different Journey

our destiny? Lao-Tzu, an ancient Chinese philosopher, said these encouraging words, "A journey of a thousand miles begins with a single step." So, what are you ducking and dodging?

If I would've allowed my pain to overshadow me by continuing to run or pretending it did not exist, I would not be the bold, confident, and powerful woman that I am today. My sisters, here me well. Please stop running from your problems. Take the initiative to fight for your future. So what if it hurts. So what if they try to take away our dignity. We won't let them destroy us. You will be amazed at what's on the inside once you decide to be still. I was flabbergasted! The new woman I'd become finally showed her true colors. Not only did I recover despite being the underdog, I learned that I could do the impossible, if I kept my head on straight. Refuse to accept what the enemy sends your way.

Exquisite Words of Wisdom

"Pain is inevitable. Suffering is optional."
Haruki Murakami

Here are eight things to do if you get sidetracked by a painful situation:

1. *Determine the cause of your pain.*
2. *Decipher how you played a role in the painful situation.*
3. *Make up your mind that you are going to get through it.*
4. *Look for opportunities, not opposition.*

5. Recite a positive affirmation for 21 days.
6. Do something nice for someone else to take your mind off it.
7. Jot down other alternatives to prevent painful anger from lingering.
8. Keep an open mind.

~Question of the Day~

When pain causes you to stop in your tracks, what can you do to get started again?

_____

_____

_____

Affirmation: During my darkest days, I refuse to stay stuck. Therefore, I will hang on to my faith and never give up.

_____

_____

_____

My afterthoughts concerning this affirmation are as follows:

_____

_____

~Goal Setting Exercise~

When pain takes me on different journey my goal for staying focused is to

_____

_____

_____

My time-frame to accomplish this goal is

_____

_____

_____

Once I have accomplished this goal, I plan to

_____

_____

_____

~Reflections to Remember~

Overcoming the Trials of Fear and Rejection

Constant rejection supersedes any motivation to explore our dreams. Consequently, it becomes next to impossible for us to leap into our destiny with our eyes wide open.

Rejection transforms into projection when we visualize the glorious future that lies ahead of us.

When we are turned down because others don't know who we really are, it behooves us to have already figured out the potential that lies on the inside. Then, no one will be mistaken.

~CHAPTER TWO~

Overcoming the Trials of Fear and Rejection

How fear and rejection can cause you to stop short of your dreams

SOMEBODY HELP ME P-L-E-A-S-E, the hopeless woman begged and pleaded, as she helplessly staggered down the ghostlike hallways of her newly built dream home. Barely able to glide her feet, her lifeless body swayed and wobbled from side to side, while sneaking towards her favorite room with blinding tears falling from her big brown puffy eyes. With splotches of thick black mascara spattered all over her made-up face, she reminded you of a spine-chilling mortal that lives in outer space. Her short, nappy hair stood up on top of her head like the spindles on a porcupine's back. I wish you could have seen her before all of *this* happened the woman was out of sight. Her jazzy lifestyle and stylish demeanor had gone from bad to worse while walking around on pins and needles as if she was going to burst.

Afraid to face the malicious crowd, she tiptoed for a while, managing to slip right past the nosy spectators. Her intentions were to avoid the nasty gossip that had the whole town talking. Of course, the curious bystanders had nothing better to do, than to make life miserable for the comfortless woman who continued to boo-hoo. Gagging and wheezing as though she had too much to drink, she stumbled towards the master suite and latched onto the wooden bed railings to keep from falling flat on her face. Nearly out of breath and insanely depressed, she clamped down firmly on the custom-made headboard, squeezing it so tightly that the warm blood circulating in her tiny wrinkled hands rushed to the end of her long pointed fingertips. Suddenly, the small veins in her sweaty palms turned black and blue while gazing out of the window wondering what in the world was she going to do.

Traumatized by the hostile critics who cold-bloodedly undermined her strength to survive, it seemed as though she would never take another step in pursuit of her dreams, visions, and intriguing aspirations. It was obvious that the jibber jabber clearly defined the troublemaker's intentions of sabotaging her life. Though the woman was usually a whiz at sorting through the bad news that nearly knocked her socks off, this time it felt as if she was beating a dead horse. The evil, irrational, and underhanded schemes that were more than just a bad dream nearly ruined her life forever.

Before she could catch her breath, the woman was virtually stunned by the disconcerting news of her marriage being on the verge of falling apart. To help relieve the tormenting pain she felt, she gently placed both hands on her wounded heart. With everything going on at once, her life was in mess, but deep down inside although she was tired, she was determined to give it her best. She thought about the domino effect this was going to have on her life, so she refused to react hastily to avoid stirring up even more strife. Somehow, through all of the chaos, she was able to think and pray, but an angelic voice kept telling her that her life could not stay that way.

In a state of shock, she thought long and hard about the possibility of going through a devastating divorce, losing her home, or even having to dissolve her successful business and leave town, if her marriage abruptly ended. Though she despised the heartache and pain that nearly pushed her over the edge, ultimately she resented the likelihood of having to start her discontented life all over again. If the disturbing news was true, at this stage of her life, how could she conceivably make it through?

Overwhelmed by a razor sharp pain in her heart her feeble body instantly collapsed onto the squeaky spacious bed. "LORD, P-L-E-A-S-E HELP ME GET THROUGH T-H-I-S," she moaned and groaned, until her throat shriveled up like a stale raisin, dry as a fried chicken bone. Simultaneously, the tears that rolled down her hollow cheeks flowed so quickly, that it actually felt like she was sitting in a stream of warm gushing water. It was obvious that she was fighting a losing battle.

The little woman continued wailing hysterically, fiercely pounding her swollen fist against the smelly pillow that was wringing wet with her salty tears. However, there wasn't anything anyone could possibly do or say in order to make her remorseful tears go away. With her head hung low, and her slender shoulders slouched forward, even a blind man could see that the heaviness of her broken heart was the crux of her bitterness, pain, and grief.

Consequently, she was apprehensive and afraid to trust anymore for fear of being rejected and tossed aside, as though she was a piece of trash. "If they had only realized the mind-blowing potential that was on the inside, they would have certainly treated her differently," she thought to herself. Though it took a while, she finally realized that she had been looking for *love* in all the wrong places, which was quite evident by the look on their mean old disgruntle faces. Finally, she tried explaining away her troubles to everyone who was there, but they threw their hands up in the air as if they did not care.

Although the woman was scared and extremely confused, she sought advice from others who may have gone through this same type of ridicule. She even thought that confiding in experts would get her life back on track, but before she could take two steps forward, those obnoxious lies knocked her right back. At times, she literally wanted to drop out of sight without even leaving a trace. Who would care, anyway, when they laughed in her face?

There were even times when she wished she could float down the drain along with the dirty sudsy water. Unfortunately, this wouldn't have solved anything, because she felt her life wasn't worth a quarter. After escaping their wicked and evil schemes, she promised that she would never look back. By this time, she was determined to do anything, just to stay on the right track. She wanted to be able to explore the world in pursuit of happiness, in hopes that the smart aleck busybodies would mind their own business.

Her ultimate desire was to empower other women to somehow find their way, but by the time she realized how messed up her own life was, all she could do was pray: *"Lord, oh Lord, I don't know what to do. Right now, my life is a wreck and it reminds me of a zoo. Sometimes, I sit and wonder; sometimes I shout and scream. Lord, oh Lord, please wake me up from this atrocious dream."*

Have you ever experienced rejection, intimidation, *and* humiliation all at once? Sounds like trouble, doesn't it? Anything that grabs our attention in a negative manner has the potential of being bad news. Rejection alone is bad enough, but when we are badgered and pushed around, like the woman you just read about, it is malicious and undermining. The searing pain that is felt as a result, is also indefensible to say the least.

It is enough to make us want to cry. Truthfully, that is an understatement. Rejection is enough to make us want to kick someone's behind, but who wants to continue wasting their precious time convincing others that they also deserve a chance to belong? Over the years, I have learned that people are going to *think* what they want to about us anyway. So is it really worth the bother?

My mother used to say, "It is the ones who are closest to us that will hurt us most." As usual, mom's ominous words were on point. She knew exactly what we needed to hear, so it really did not take me by surprise when she became very assertive in the middle of an unpleasant conversation that required a little guidance from an adult. One of her favorite things to do was to share her experiences with my siblings and me, hoping to deter us from the fiery darts of those wicked people who tried to make us look bad or minimize our self-worth. She was never one who would give us the run-around. There were no surprises if my mom had anything to do with it. She was up front with anything she had to say.

Mom was not about to pass up a good opportunity to get her momentous point across. One thing for sure, her occasional lectures provided powerful, yet practical life lessons which represented "the law of the land" in our house. Once she started speaking, we could usually gage whether or not she was going to be rather chatty by her tone of voice or the presumptuous look she gave us right before she laid it on the line.

My mother was the type of person who would save the world from getting marred by life's cruelties if she could. So we had better be prepared to sit and listen. She was certainly going to speak her mind and dared us to fall asleep or part our lips in rebellion. No one could stop her from getting down to the real nitty-gritty, not even my eldest sister, Sheila, who was in charge of the family when our parents were away at work.

Unfortunately, this time, the pain of rejection and fear of the unknown that brought me to my knees, was a bit much for mom's insightful words. When someone steals your heart and breaks it in two, it is only a matter of time before a host of negative emotions set in. It seems as though they just pop up out of nowhere causing us to be irrational beings. If these adverse feelings hang around long enough, love turns into hatred, hatred produces anger, and anger breeds war. All hell breaks loose. Rage is inevitable. Some of us see another side of us that we never knew existed until our pain piggybacks on our emotions and the bottom falls out. The language that accidentally slips out of our mouths would definitely put a sailor to shame. This is the way that it is when we are forsaken by a loved one. Our gut reactions are impossible to ignore when someone gives us the thumbs down on more than one occasion. For this reason, our confidence goes out the window and it is more than a notion trying to gain it back.

How could I have *not* seen it coming when everyone else around me noticed the red flags waving from the eastern shore? Was I *that* oblivious to the fact that he really did not love me anymore? Regardless of the circumstances, I had to get my life together, so I began focusing on "me" and not any other fellow. Now I am able to give sound advice to women all over the land. I used the strength I had within, without depending on any other man. *JEHOVAH RAPHA,* the Lord Who Heals, put an end to my insufferable pain. I am humbled by His faithfulness, and because of Him, I am no longer ashamed.

There are many ways to define rejection. Charles R. Solomon, author of *The Rejection Syndrome,* puts it this way: "Rejection is the absence of meaningful love." We all have an inbred need to feel loved even if it is only for a moment. When women experience rejection, we take it to heart. We do not like to ha-ha or make wisecracks about anything that is degrading to us. Nine times out of ten, it rips our hearts in two. Furthermore, it makes us look like a fool. The opportunity to experience rejection is always present when there is a strong desire for affection. In order for there to be a positive connection between two individuals, the feeling must be mutual. There has to be something that clicks, or at least something that makes your heart flutters, when the person comes around. Either one will definitely ignite a string of positive emotions that are not easily turned off. Generally, when two people do not share the same vibes, rejection is the monster that causes anxiety, fear, and hopelessness.

Rejection is also characterized, as the act of pushing someone away, or turning our backs on them when we have failed to conquer our own prejudices. Because the radars in our brain cells are always on the lookout, we automatically back off, having nothing to do with the person. Their unpleasant traits easily get under our skin when we do not want to be bothered. Consequently, we come to a hasty decision based on erroneous assumptions.

The motivation behind rejection in some instances is that we are quick to scope out the flaws of others merely based on first impressions. Sometimes, what you see is *not* what you get. By all means, I am certainly aware that first impressions have a lasting effect on us, but if our hunches turn out to be misconstrued, why do we still hang on to them? For years, we have conditioned our minds to focus on the negative aspects of others, but why aren't we brave enough to tell a person what it was that prompted us to feel that way? Our boldness could actually help. Instead, we use some lame excuse as a cover up hoping to smooth them over.

We don't give each other enough credit. What do you think is going to happen if we told someone the truth? Will we get our brains beaten out or something? I do not believe this will be the case if we learn to just tell the truth and let them handle it. Yet, we won't say how we truly feel, but we will try to dictate how the other person should react when we cast them aside. Does that make any sense at all?

For the most part, we fail to recognize the potential of others when we count them out right off the bat, without giving them a chance to prove us wrong. Certainly, there are countless good qualities in us all, it just depends of whose looking. Some people will make it their business to zero in on the quirks and idiosyncrasies of others, while ignoring their own strange irregularities. In some of us, these qualities are so great that sometimes they're simply overlooked. All it takes is for someone to rub us the wrong way and we let him (or her) have it. We denounce them and even go as far as excluding them from our lives, sometimes for good.

Rejection is a "biggie" in terms of our craving for acceptance the older we become as women. We long for companionship. When it does not happen as quickly as we would like, we start kicking and screaming even pulling our hair out. Unfortunately, some of us live our lives by the way people treat us, so rejection *does* have a significant impact. At the same time, it is totally up to us how we handle the repercussion. We can allow what others say or do to us to cause us not to reach our destiny or we can take the high road and accomplish our dreams in spite of what they say. According to James Lee Burke, an American author of mysteries, "There's nothing like rejection to make you do an inventory of yourself."

Rejection can have an adverse effect on how we picture ourselves when we are insecure or feel threatened. Although rejection is not a good feeling by a long shot, we should not allow it to interfere with our happiness or our destiny in life. Easier said than done, right? However, for the most part, rejection is not an easy thing to shove aside in the corner somewhere and pretend that it never really happened. Then again, most of us do just that. We never deal with the hurt so we meander through life harboring unnecessary pain. Henceforth, it becomes nearly impossible to accomplish our dreams when all we think about day in and day out is how someone has shot us down or brushed us off because they never took time out to get to know us.

When we experience rejection, I guarantee that someone else besides us will know about it. It isn't something that can be easily kept under wraps; at least not for long. It is bothersome and downright hurtful when limitations are set on us because people do not believe that we have what it takes. John 15:18 clearly warns us about the possibility of experiencing rejection. It says it this way, *"If the world hates you, keep in mind that it hated me first"* (NIV). This biblical principle prepares us for rejection long before we experience it firsthand. When it does happen to us, we will be equipped to handle it like a champion if we keep these words tucked away in our hearts.

My friend, the Lord truly wants to heal us from the arduous pain of rejection that can cause us to fall short of our dreams. Jeremiah 29:11 says it like this: *"For I know the plans I have for you; declares the Lord, plans to prosper you and not to harm you, plans to give you hope and a future"* (NIV). No matter what we have to endure, when we hear of promises like *that,* we should automatically draw closer to the one who can certainly make good on them and will not kick us to the curve. The Lord will never shun us aside nor will He push us away, in fact, just the opposite. He welcomes us with His arms wide open.

Social rejection in particular, is one of the worst feelings we will ever experience, specifically, for those of us who are treated like an outcast, by someone very near and dear. A close friend, a relative, or a beloved spouse is not someone who automatically comes to mind when we think of rejection. Researchers across the nation have found that rejection can hurt just as much as being physically injured. Ouch. "As far as the brain is concerned, a broken heart may not be so different from a broken arm,"[1] according to Kirsten Weir, author of *Science Watch*. Weir further explains that, "Like hunger or thirst, our need for acceptance emerged as a mechanism for survival. The truth is that regardless of how much we try to make ourselves believe that we don't need people in our lives, there will always be an opportunity that is bound to prove us wrong."[2]

Anyone, who has experienced rejection in the past, can tell you that it feels as if their heart literally skipped a beat. To begin with, "rejection is a cacophony of emotions in your head that make you feel and wish would just shut up somehow." These emotions may include frustration, anger, disappointment, and futility. Charles Matthew, a well-versed writer, believes that rejection is the worst pain a human being can ever experience, but never explain. More than that, "rejection is like every bone in your body crumbles, every muscle spasms and every sense in your body disappears."

Another key point is that rejection is used as a smoke-screen, when we do not want to tell someone that they are not good enough, or that there is something about them that doesn't quite add up. Add up to what, though, and who's counting anyway? Do we really stand out like a sore thumb if our lives are out of sync with everybody else's? Although this seems to be the case, we were *all* born with differences. Our differences make us unique. In fact, there is nothing wrong with being exceptional, extraordinary, or one-of-a-kind. These are all unprecedented attributes that can carry us a long way if we use them to our advantage without allowing others to make us feel badly because of who we are. Shame on them; not us.

Wait a minute. Let's take our time and think about this for a moment before we get all bent out of shape. Most times, when we experience rejection, it is not always about us, per say, although that does not make it any easier for the other party on the receiving end. With that in mind, we should breathe a sigh of relief, despite the difficulty of even cracking a smile when someone has intentionally hurt us. When all is said and done and the real reason for the exclusion is exposed, we often find that it was the individual who tried excluding us from his (or her) social circle that was the problem—not us. We were merely recipients of their ruthless actions and it hurts us to the core.

I can certainly attest to the fact that rejection causes damage to our psyche. When I was going through my hard times and my world was in shambles, I could have sworn that rejection was my middle name. It seemed as though I could not fit in anywhere, or could it have been that those around me would not let me in? Unfortunately, it remains that way today. For some reason, I still find myself trying to run with the crowd and often wind up getting my feelings crushed. I can't imagine that they would not welcome me into their circle or even invite me to have lunch with the crew, based on a technicality. Initially, I thought there was something wrong with me, but after realizing who I am in the Lord, their silly little games don't bother me as much. I refuse to give them that satisfaction.

Everyone feels the need to belong. Human beings strive for acceptance. Hence, we constantly try to appease others. We even try to wiggle our way into a multitude of cliques, to put our minds at ease, when we are antsy about being alone. It is sad to admit, but while growing up, I was one who tried to buy friendship. I did this in order to be a part of what was known then, as the "in crowd." My actions made my father furious when he heard that I was giving away his hard-earned money. He jumped all over me. He even hooped and hollered as loud as he could to deter me from this type of unacceptable behavior.

Nevertheless, the sound of his tumultuous voice did not scare me one bit; I wanted to belong. Dad was not the one who was missing out on the fun, so it was easy for him to give advice from the outside looking in. What he did not understand was that I wanted to be with my friends. Anyway, dad never succeeded, so eventually he gave up trying, but in the end, I was the one who ended up crying.

You are probably thinking to yourself that there is no way on earth you would have tried winning someone over by giving up your most valuable items. On the other hand, I did not want to feel like an outcast either. Back in the day that wasn't cool. If you were not a part of the group, people thought something was terribly wrong with you. They made a point of letting you know it too.

Rejection can be tough when it seems that everyone else is head over heels in love except us. We are perturbed and even beside ourselves when we can't seem to make heads or tails out of it. All we know is that we have something eating away at us on the inside that just won't quit. The voice of rejection keeps playing in our minds that we are undesirable, unwanted, and unwelcomed, but if that was true what type of person would that make me or you?

Are you aware that rejection can cause heartbreak, which also has an enormous effect on our appetites? Debra Smouse, co-author of the article, *The Breakup Diet: Why Heartbreak Affects Our Appetite* believes that, while many people turn to eating when they break-up with their loved ones to alleviate the pain, others may not want to eat at all. Smouse stated that, "It's as if there is a connection between our stomachs and our hearts, and any food that crosses our lips sends us into pain. We're unable to swallow. We force ourselves to eat something, and it immediately comes back up. Though we aren't ready to feel healing and hope, we don't desire to feel any more pain. So, we abstain from eating."[3]

Furthermore, if we eat too much when we are depressed it can be harmful. If we do not eat at all, it can be detrimental. It seems like a no-win situation. On the other hand, a warm and fuzzy reception will more than likely boost our self-confidence. This makes us feel more valuable as women. Women, who have experienced rejection, will most likely agree that it is very degrading when someone crosses us off their list. When we are intentionally ignored, or told that our opinions do not matter, it can have an adverse psychological effect on us as well. More than that, constant rejection can get under our skin like a rare fungus that has no scientific cure. The results can be lethal. What's even worse is when women experience rejection for no rhyme or reason as I did.

Do you remember the deplorable little woman that you read about early on in the chapter? Well, that was me. That's right; little old me. However, I managed to pick up the pieces and start my life all over again, leaning on the Lord every step of the way. Without Him by my side, I could not have made it another day. Make no bones about it, *that* whirlwind of uncertainty was nothing to play with. To be perfectly honest with you that was the worst transitional period of my life. I had to sign over my dream home during the divorce proceedings, relocate to a city where I knew no one, and close the business that was established as a source of retirement income, but I made it through all of that and then some. These major events alone would send even the healthiest person to an early grave.

I know you might be saying to yourself that my situation was no different then what other women would have done if they were in my shoes. Unfortunately, the odds of surviving such a nightmare were next to none. Not only did I have to withstand the travesty of being publically humiliated due to my tragic circumstances that almost left me destitute, but the rug was snatched right out from under me during one the most inopportune times of my life; the death of my beloved mother. How could someone ever recover from something as pernicious as *that?* Moreover, how could anyone conceivably plan for a proper homegoing service for the woman who brought them into this world? How could you even channel your mind to think straight? In my case, I couldn't. My dear mother went to her grave thinking that her baby girl was doing just fine. Unfortunately, it was all a lie. My life had been turned upside down and the woman she once knew would *never* be the same. So, what do you do when something like that forces you to your knees while trying to hold back the tears of misery and shame? I did the most logical thing that came to mind. I put my trust in the Lord. Today, I'm still trusting in Him.

I would love to hear my mother's soft-spoken voice again. Her ceaseless words of wisdom wowed my deepest intuition and the aroma of her delicious homemade peach cobblers and freshly cooked collard greens will forever fill my nostrils. At times, I still feel as though I was cheated out of having an opportunity to mourn my mother's death. Worse than that, I was *almost* cheated out of life itself.

Boy, how time flies. I can remember when it happened, as if it was just yesterday. There was a perfectly peaceful look on my mother's face when she took her last breath. She was tired of going through all of the pain, so why wouldn't she have left? Mom gave of herself and reached out to others whenever there was a need. Oh, how I love her and miss her so much; she was warrior and my best friend indeed.

Can you imagine carrying around something as tragic as *that* for that length of time? Sis, it's a wonder I did not lose my mind. If I told you my story a thousand times, you still might not believe that it's true. After experiencing something as devastating as *that;* I don't look like what I have been through.

When things hit me in the face all at once, I realized that I needed to put my faith into action. Hebrews 11:6 says it like this; *"But without faith it is impossible to please Him, for he who comes to God must believe that He is, and that He is a rewarder of those who diligently seek Him"* (NKJV). There was nowhere else for me to turn, but to the Lord. He brought me through the trials of fear and rejection victoriously. He was able to put my life back together so that the whole world could see.

Now that I have had a taste of rejection and loneliness, I can somewhat relate to those who are homeless. One day I was living in a decent place, then moments later, I did not know where I was going to end up. Something like that can give us the shock of our lives, and that is exactly what happened to me. It was the fear of the unknown that irritated me most and scared me out of my wits, but I knew I had to keep it moving, although it was the pits.

The only thing that kept me from giving up was that I was determined not to allow my hardships to rob me of the glorious future that the Lord had in store for me. What an awesome friend to have by my side who loves me unconditionally. Another reason why I had to survive that shockingly painful mess was that deep down inside I wanted to stay alive, and I figured that it was only a test.

As you can plainly see, certain aspects of my life story are probably very similar to yours, if not a carbon copy. This is one reason why I am passionate about sharing my story with you. No one can begin to imagine how hopeless and groveling I felt after going through those weary days and lonely nights. Believe it or not, the pain still resonates in my heart as I bleed inwardly from the residue of many unwarranted scars.

It took some growing pains for me to get to where I am right now. THANK GOD ALMIGHTY I made it through somehow. Jesus said it this way; *"I have told you these things, so that in me you may have peace. In this world, you will have trouble. But take heart. I have overcome the world"* (John 16:33, NIV). Not only did He fight my battles; He gave me my life back, girl.

Before I bring this chapter to a close there are just a few more things that I would like for you to know. When all *hell* has broken loose; don't run around in circles like a wild mother goose. When your dreams have been shattered and have vanished in the night; don't sit around saying you're too tired to fight. You've prayed and waited and waited and prayed; so don't give up now your dreams are only delayed. Though your life seems to be headed in the opposite direction, stop telling yourself you need some love and affection. You must do better before it gets worst. Get it together my sister or you are going to burst.

Your future is on the line, so you better make haste. Take my hand and hold on tight; we don't have time to waste. There are many painful misfortunes, we face on a daily basis, but we must persevere and never stand still in order to change places. So don't you give up *hope* and start depending on others. Don't even waste your time by depending on a brother.

You can change your present situation before it's all too late. If you start right now, my sister, things will turn out GREAT. If you see yourself as others see you during your time of distress, you will *never* get it together my dear, or pass those grueling tests. Be encouraged my sister. If I did it, you can too. P-L-E-A-S-E do not allow rejection to stop you from being you.

Exquisite Words of Wisdom

"Often you think when you've been rejected that you are not good enough, but the truth is they weren't ready for all you have to offer." Author Unknown

Here are seven ways to overcome rejection in order to accomplish your dreams:

1. Do not let rejection get you down.
2. Refuse to dwell on it.
3. Focus on what you have to offer.
4. Hang out with those who accept you for who you are.
5. Use rejection as a means of enhancing your personal qualities.
6. Research the real reasons why some people reject others. Knowledge is power.
7. Consider the source.

~QUESTION of the DAY~

We have all experienced rejection in some form or fashion. Most times, we cannot figure out why. What can you do to alleviate those ill feelings associated with rejection when it happens to you?

_____

_____

_____

_____

Affirmation: I will not allow fear and rejection to engulf me. I am an overcomer.

My afterthoughts concerning this affirmation are as follows:

_____

_____

_____

~Goal Setting Exercise~

My goal for conquering fear and rejection is to

_____

_____

_____

My time-frame to accomplish this goal is

_____

_____

_____

Once I have accomplished this goal, I plan to_

_____

_____

~Reflections to Remember~

Giants do Fall

The giants in our lives will never know how much we fear them if we do not disclose it ourselves. What comes out of our mouths can actually destroy us.

Most of our giants only impose a threat when we see them as larger than life. Having a false image of what our problems will do to us causes unnecessary anxiety.

If we look at things differently, giants are bullish creatures. They force us into doing the impossible, when no one else thought it was possible.

~CHAPTER THREE~

Giants do Fall

How to slay the "giants" in your life

Everywhere you go these days people are talking about giants. They are sick and tired of the annoying barbarian beasts. You would think the voluminous monsters roam the earth both day and night, but that depends on who is doing the talking. Do giants really wander about with a wooden beat-up stick in their hands walloping and clobbering anything in sight? Well, according to the grapevine, they do. Unfortunately, some of us believe *everything* that we hear. So, before we get all worked up over nothing, let us dig a little bit deeper to determine what the hairy monsters are really made of. In times of distress, people see things that do not exist, you know. Our worries could soon be over.

For years, the only giants that I ever read about were the ones that had a monster-like appearance and supernatural powers. In a world of people with average heights, giants seemed exceptionally tall and resembled historic cavemen. They were also gigantic creatures with huge muscles and extraordinary strength. From the sound of it, giants were unfriendly, unusual, and very unpredictable. Those ferocious-looking beasts appeared strong and intimidating. Most people would not go near the Herculean creature because they were afraid of being devoured, *but* could it have been the other way around? Is it possible that the monstrous Cyclops was actually afraid of them?

Interestingly enough there is another giant that poses an eminent threat. However, this "giant" is also overruling. In the minds of those who have had an unpleasant encounter with the huge critter, its personality is identical to that of the imaginary monster that supposedly had everybody running for their lives back in the day. Although we were inclined to believe those tales were a bunch of nonsense, somewhere in the back of our minds the legendary mammoth still exists. In fact, it has no respect of persons. As reported by some of its victims who barely survived the merciless attacks, "it is going to take an army to lay this sucker to rest."

In this chapter, I intend to hammer away at those beastly monsters that appear out of nowhere and take us down by the throat. After all, someone has to go toe to toe with the hellion. Without further ado, I am tossing my hat into the ring, so let's get started. We have wasted enough time with our heads on the chopping block. Now it's time for us to do the chopping.

For the record, the werewolf that I am alluding to is *not* the "jolly green giant" with the shiny sparkling smile and curly green hair. He is the one who tries his best to persuade us to eat his brand of healthy and nutritious veggies. Thank goodness, the famous television character is not as bad as he appears. Frankly, he is quite the opposite. At any rate, "giants" are anything or anybody who has a stronghold on us. Simply put, pesky problems and pretentious people are considered giants that grab hold of our emotions. The people with whom we live or work are sometimes giants when they try to take control of our lives. When our adult children decide to move back in with us or our spouses go for a joyride at 2:00am every morning, these are both monsters we dread facing. More than that, an empty bank account when the rent is past due is a monstrosity in itself.

The mere thought of a giant controlling our lives scare some of us half to death. When we are afraid of something or someone fear sends us a distress signal that danger is nearby. Some of the apparent signs of nervousness may include rapid heartbeats, sweaty body parts, extremely large eyes, and stomach sickness. Fear is a whale of a problem although there is usually some good that comes out of it. It wakes us up to the potential that something could possibly harm us. Comparatively, worrying make us feel unsafe and unsure. It prepares us for what is ahead, one way or another. Fear and worrying, gets us fired up about unpleasant events that can potentially wipe us out. Not being able to survive those unexpected attacks is our biggest worry.

Sometimes, when we face uncertainty and fear it can be a nail-biting experience, which causes us to get the heebie-jeebies when we do not know where we are going to end up next. That's spooky. Those wearisome moments can also cause the more than one hundred thousand strands of hair on our head to stand up at its roots. I hate to be the bearer of bad news, but before you leave this earth, you *will* also come face to face with a giant that is difficult for you to slay. Disturbingly, if you do not have the right weapons at your disposal you *are* going to lose, but in all honesty, who wants to be at such disadvantage before the fight even begins? What an appalling place to be. If you are lucky enough not to have to face a giant today, tomorrow is only a few hours away. Just remember, the victor is always the one who is left standing when the war is finally over. It behooves *you* to be the one standing.

Over time, our unexpected giants *can* be detrimental the more we try avoiding them. When we are overwhelmed, naturally, we try sweeping those problems that give us headaches under the carpet as though they never really existed. We lie to ourselves to avoid facing the truth because it hurts. Face it. It's embarrassing and demeaning to admit we have a serious problem when it boils down to believing in ourselves. Some of us don't believe that we have what it takes to kill the giants in our lives, but that doesn't mean that we *never* will. Simply put, fear has us on the run.

We do more harm than good when we panic before we give ourselves a chance. That is how some of us coast through life when we are petrified of our problems. We act as though we are afraid to open our mouths. Therefore, we go around murmuring and silently complaining to ourselves, but where has all of the silence and frustration gotten us when our giants have refused to leave us alone? I can certainly think of a few choice words. However, since *our* giants are not always identical, and what bothers you might not bother me, you will have the pleasure of deciding this factor for yourself. I have learned that giants *do* die and "the bigger they are, the harder they fall."

Life presents us with some hard knocks when we doubt our capabilities. It is my prayer that the lessons you walk away with from this chapter will be very similar to the ones I've learned over time. Although they were difficult, they helped to make me the woman I am today.

Come closer, as I shed a little light on some of the uncanny accusations or *giants*, if you will, that inspired me to write this book. In addition to the aspirations I spoke of in the introduction, it is my desire to empower women to take a stand against what is eating away at us, consequently, hindering us from enjoying our lives just like everybody else. Why does it seem as though we are always catching hell? I believe our problem is that, in some instances, we open ourselves up for others to take advantage when we are closed-minded and vulnerable. We are closed-minded when we refuse to think outside the box. To be vulnerable is to, "risk being wounded, not just emotionally, but being subject to criticism, moral scrutiny or temptation, as in a point of weakness," according to William Butler, author of the book, *Be Love to Others*.

Butler further implies that being vulnerable means that you are without protection "like a sitting duck" that is wide open for the kill. In addition, when trouble comes our way, we act like basket cases during the most inopportune times. Some of us just give up too easily. We don't know what we are really made of because we were afraid to fight. The enemy knows that all it takes is for someone to look at us the wrong way and we are inundated with fear to the point that we can't function properly. Our knees knock and legs shake. We tremble at the thought of losing. When we give our giants free reign to walk all over us, what do you think is going to happen? We will be smashed and crushed even battered and bruised. Some of us might be left for dead. I was guilty of giving up until I learned how to fight without wearing myself thin. I learned to fight sensibly by allowing the Lord to do it instead. He knows how to get the job done.

The key to surviving a potentially deadly attack, orchestrated by our giants, is *not* to allow our vulnerability to get in the way by thinking with our *hearts* instead of our *heads*. We are famous for doing that. Most of us are girly-girly and extremely good-natured at the wrong time. In addition, we are soft-hearted and easy-going when a situation calls for us to dig our heels in. There is no middle ground when a giant has our backs up against the wall. It is hard for us to win and lose at the same time. Something has got to give, preferably in our favor.

If you are reading this chapter with great intensity, that probably means you are experiencing some degree of depression and hopelessness, which are the same aggravating feelings that nearly caused me to give up on life. At one of my lowest points, I was falsely accused of saying things that I did not say, doing things that I did not do, and starting things that I certainly did not start. It appeared as though the finger pointing was always at me. For a while, some even labeled me as somewhat of an instigator or "a person who loved to stir the pot and run" which could not be further from the truth, talking about a "giant" especially when those false accusations came directly from the people who were very close to me.

Despite the thinning and proving, I was still misunderstood, and no matter how hard I tried clearing my name, would you believe it got even worse? Of course, their rigid jaws, tensed faces, and tight lips warned me that they did not want to hear a word I had to say. Isn't it funny how our loved ones can be so fickle at times? They are supposed to have our backs. No one expects for *them* to side with the enemy. In some cases, *they* have become the enemy.

Subsequently, when the slanderous remarks kept coming my way, agitation and tension led to feelings of inadequacy, insecurity, and powerlessness. If those wisecracks were an indication of the "giants" that were headed my way, I definitely needed a flawless plan of attack in place. You think that was crazy, it was also said that, "I was a person of double standards," which meant to those doing the judging that I said one thing, but did another. Once again, that was not me at all—far from it. That just goes to show you that people who thought they knew me really didn't. The undeserved bashing directed towards me could have easily led to poor judgment and wayward thinking on my behalf if I would have overreacted emotionally, but I knew better. My parents taught me during my younger days when to keep my mouth shut. Believe me; I had plenty of practice.

To further illustrate my point, the defamatory statements and malicious condemnation that you hear of happening to others actually happened to me, the woman who had it all together, according to the world's eye view. However, the world's favorable opinion of me could not prevent the gnawing pain from ripping my heart in two. Here's another scenario that almost caused me to lose it. On my way home from church one day, I was also in such state of shock that my mouth flew wide open in disbelief when false rumors started spreading here, there, and everywhere.

The one that nearly did me in was when I was thrown into the category of "someone who was all for self" but you had to be totally out of your mind to believe something like that. Some even said that I had an overwhelming desire for more so they attached the word "greed" to my name for no apparent reason. In my own defense, I have always been the kind of person who would give to anyone in need, so it was not about greed, as some wanted you to believe. Had I continued listening to those who tried to rake me over the coals, I would have lost my mind defending myself, and guess what? It wasn't even worth it. This was another typical example of a giant in pursuit of defaming my character.

Well, if that didn't take the cake, some of my acquaintances had the nerve to say that I would "run scared at the drop of a hat" or "develop cold feet if I had to stand up to anyone when trouble came knocking at my door." Frankly, I did not feel the need to argue, fuss, and fight—so why should they? My focus was essentially on getting my life back together after a horrible divorce that left me feeling barren, broken, and useless. My desire was to become a brand *new* me, relentless, to be exact. I had sense enough to know that a huge investment was in the making and I was not about to let anyone ruin it for me, not this time.

On the other hand, the sad part about the statement that singled me out as being a capricious individual was the truth, so I couldn't give those who said it a piece of my mind, which I felt like doing, but was too scared to even open my mouth. The backstabbing jargon was literally stressing me out, which in turn, led to other health related issues that I concealed from everyone I knew. Once again, I had to keep my mouth shut so that my ill-will contenders would not know my every move. This is how I outsmarted my enemies. Sometimes, talking too much *can* be fatal.

Clearly, my emotions were running wild which stemmed from allowing others to walk all over me. In essence, I was a "people pleaser" but of course, I tried hiding it. I was very good at "putting on a happy face." When I was home alone behind closed doors my mind was all over the place. Then, one day, reality slapped this girl in the face when I recalled one of my mother's famous life lessons. She told me that I could not get angry with someone if he (or she) was speaking the truth about me. Then, with a stern look on her face, she took it a step further, by adding, "If you don't like what's being said; do something about it." What she really meant was that it was time for me to make a change. Although I my feelings were crushed, I had to agree.

At that moment, I realized that I may not be able to stop every repulsive "giant" that came my way, but it made good sense to own up to my hang-ups, since everybody has them, and move forward. I can also remember being afraid of any and everything, so to speak. If someone said, "boo" you bet I would jump, so the tendencies of being an individual who was nervous and faint-hearted were certainly present. One thing for sure, you could never tell it by the cheery look on my face. I mastered all the right moves that had everybody fooled, so I thought. Considering everything that was going on with me, I knew someday I had to conqueror those giants in order for me to become a woman who could stand on her own two feet. Today, I can proudly say that I am that woman. I am pleased to meet you.

Let me paint an even clearer picture that will persuade you to take a stand against those troublesome giants that are bound to destroy your life if you let them. Only *you* can change the direction your life is going. No one else can do it for you. Joyce Meyer, an awesome minister and *New York Times* bestselling author, made it as plain as day when she said to the crowd of attendees at one of her revitalizing seminars: "You are stronger than you think you are especially in the face of fear." Her point was well taken. We never know what is on the inside of us until we are under pressure to perform. Amazingly, while sweating bullets we can do the impossible if we believe we can. We can even move mountains created by others to kill us when we are focused. Most of us can write a book about our own experiences if we had to. Trust me; I will never forget those convincing words that caused me to think twice. I often say them to myself whenever I am in the middle of a crisis. They seem to get me through it every time.

Speaking of a deadlock situation, there was a time in my adult life where I felt like a prisoner in my own home. I couldn't do this and I couldn't do that. Likewise, I couldn't touch this and I couldn't touch that. Although I resided in a home that represented "The American Dream," I did not feel as though I could thrive in a place where literally everything I said or did was scrutinized and intentionally shot down by those living under the same roof. It was sheer torture. If I breathed the wrong way, my life was made a living hell by the guy who said, "I do." Can anyone tell me what type of relationship would flourish under those taxing conditions? By the way, why was the evil-minded treatment necessary from the get-go? Honestly, some people are just mean and nasty for no reason. Misery loves company. Nevertheless, I had to conform for the sake of keeping peace. On the other hand, I was planning to get out of there like a wild frantic beast.

There is nothing worse than constantly walking on eggshells in the confines of your own home. What is even more sickening was that for years, I was afraid to grab hold of the lifeline that could have pulled me safely to shore. Yet, I remained in bondage for years, until I decided that there was more to life than showing what you know behind closed doors. That was a lot of time being wasted feeling lonely, incomplete, and chasing after unfilled dreams. If you think about it, fourteen years is longer than some individuals have been gainfully employed.

It is a shame when we go through life without reaching for the key that unleashes our future when it is hanging right in front of our faces. I knew there was a better life out there somewhere for me once I got over the initial fear and anxiety of being alone. At the time, I could not see it nor did I have the strength to go after it. What an alarming situation that was. To make matters worse, my darling mother of eighty-four years had just passed away. Her death left the family with many decisions to make on behalf of my elderly father, who was as ornery as he could be. Though he meant well, everyone could tell it was *not* going to be easy, but me.

Shortly afterwards, my marriage fell apart, which meant that I had to hustle to find a decent place to live until I could pull it all together. In the midst of the craziness, my educational business that enhanced the academic lives of many children and adults took a serious nosedive, leaving me alone and scrambling to find another place of employment in the area. This was totally out of my comfort zone after having worked two jobs for the majority of my life. What the heck, it was do-or-die. During those distressful times, I could not afford to have a cavalier attitude. I would have taken the first thing that I could get my hands on if it meant keeping my head above water. Ladies, this is what happens to us when we get into desperate situations. Our giants overpower us. We do not know which way to go or what we are going to do. That is why I can easily say that sometimes our lives remind us of a zoo.

There were times when I thought I was not going to make it, but I was determined to keep on trucking even if I had to fake it. My nights were lonely, dark, cold, and rough. That is when I realized that I had to be tough. I am not saying that I was mean, grouchy, and could not ask for help. What I am telling you is that I had to TOUGHEN UP. I did so many things I did not want to do. Most people would say, "She sure was a fool." If they were in my shoes, they would be running too. This is why you cannot let everyone tell you what to do.

Here's my point: what tends to hurt us most is that we allow ourselves to be constrained by others who mean us no good when we do not lift a finger to do anything about it. We willingly hand over the reins in order to satisfy someone else's authoritarian temperament, which is their problem not ours. Some of us roll over and play dead, consequently, never using our weapons of courage, faith, audacity, and resilience. We need to rise up and say to Goliath, "You are dying." Being in control of our giants is a good thing, since we have become accustomed to dancing to the beat of everyone's drum except for our own. Now it's time to dance to a different tune, ours.

Moreover, we sit back and cross our legs without taking a stand for what we believe is the right thing for us to do. This seems like a *normal* occurrence for some. How is it possible to know our strength if we never get out of our normal? However, if we get out of our normal, we will find out what we are truly made of. All of us have been there; some of us are still there. Have you ever wondered why we did not take hold of the key that was dangling right in front of us and unlock the door? Moreover, why did we *not* run like heck when we discovered that the door was already open? Could it be that we were scared stiff of those irritating giants or were we simply unequipped for the battle? When I made up mind that I had to do something totally different to survive, I started believing in myself, one accomplishment at a time.

There will be times when we will go through unwarranted and crushing circumstances that we wish would magically disappear. It would be even better if we could wave a golden wand in front of our faces or from side to side. Wouldn't that be nice? Abracadabra—poof!—all of our problems would vanish into the great blue yonder. We could then go about our merry little way. This sounds like a plan, doesn't it? Well, I do not mean to burst your bubble, but it doesn't work like that at all. Facing those annoying giants take tremendous strength, coupled with an amazing strategy. Slaying them *will* take a miracle. Jesus Christ, our Savior, will show up in time to help us triumph over our giants. That is what I call miraculous.

All of us, me included, will need a helping hand with our Goliaths at some point. Although we *think* we know what it will take to resolve our problems, we must first acknowledge that they exist. Acknowledging that our quandaries can be overwhelmingly devastating is another ideal way of handling them. Once we are able to take it all in, we *must* get down to the root of those bad situations before they end tragically. I have heard of some women falling off the deep end because they could not get a handle on their giants. They have given up on the *one* who could easily solve their problems, or given up on life period. Either way it is tragic.

Subsequently, those piercing accusations, or giants, usually have a negative connotation on us as women. Can you tell me why we continuously allow this to happen to us? WE ARE NOT HAVING THAT. Enough is enough. Hasn't that happened to you more than you would have wanted it to already? By the way, aren't you tired of living your life like a puppet on a string and doing the same old thing? Our lives are a precious gift from the Lord, not to mention that He died on the cross so that we could live eternally with Him. What an awesome gift He gave you and me, but if you do not take your life back right now, you'll remain in misery. I intend to help you, my sister, to stay on the right track so that when things start looking pretty good for you, you will *never* want to go back.

In closing, we are constrained by our own perceived failures that are not as they appear. Most of the giants we face are set in motion to harm us, but actually if we play our cards right they help us to become a better person. Some of us would not even know the magnitude of our strength if it were not for the trouble that comes our way. If we look at our problems from a different angle, there is a very strong possibility that we will heighten our awareness of what we can do or become when we are in hot water.

On the contrary, we just cannot seem to get past the "giants" for fear of being gobbled up. Subsequently, we find ourselves "shaking in our boots" because our lives have been plagued with uncertainty and fear. Here's the trick: if we overcome the fear, we conquer the "giant." If you really want to know the truth "that which we are afraid of is actually afraid of us." Which "giants" are holding you hostage and preventing you from bouncing back? Break out from under their manipulation and control. Start living a fearless life today. Giants do fall, but honey, *don't* let them fall on you.

Exquisite Words of Wisdom

Before you begin any adventure, always remember to pray for guidance. Here is one of my favorite:

> *"God, grant me the serenity to accept the things I cannot change, the courage to change the things I can, and wisdom to know the difference." Reinhold Niebuhr*

Here are eleven things you can do to help defeat the "giants" in your life.

1. Acknowledge that you have a huge problem. Ownership demonstrates courage.
2. Ask yourself, "Why is there a need for change?"
3. Be willing to let go of anger and fear. They only escalate the problem.
4. Make up your mind that you are going to forgive no matter what.
5. Imagine the shoe on the other foot. Try to embrace the problem from another perspective.
6. Write down S.M.A.R.T. Plans (A and B).
7. S-Safe, M-Moral, A-Adaptable, R-Risk-taking, and T-Therapeutic
8. Talk to at least three other spiritually mature people.
9. Model how you will implement your plan before moving forward.
10. Work up a sweat prior to confronting your "giants." Sweating helps to relieve stress.

11. *If Plan A does not work, wait 3 days and implement Plan B.*

~Question of the Day~

How will you handle the "giants" that continue to show up out of nowhere?

_____

_____

_____

_____

Affirmation: Any "giant" that comes my way today is in for a real treat. I am going to welcome it with open arms. My actions will be totally unexpected.
My afterthoughts concerning this affirmation are as follows:

_____

_____

_____

_____

~Goal Setting Exercise~

My goal for slaying the "giants" in my life is to

_____

_____

_____

_____

My time-frame to accomplish this goal is

_____

_____

_____

_____

Once I have accomplished this goal, I plan to_

_____

_____

_____

_____

~Reflections to Remember~

What to do When You're Feeling Hopeless

The greatness within us lies in the power to turn someone else's life around without having their permission. Just do it.

Hopelessness can easily transform into joy if we sacrificially give of ourselves to others even when we do not see anything in it for us.

Random acts of kindness build character, especially when we are not trying to draw attention to ourselves.

~CHAPTER FOUR~

What to do When You're Feeling Hopeless

How doing the unexpected can change your life for good

Individuals experience hopelessness for a number of reasons. Insecurity and self-doubt are among the primary causes. These troubling emotions are all too common in people who are often sad and depressed. At the same time, depression casts a dark shadow in the lives of those of us who are heavyhearted and down in the dumps. When we wrestle with these bewildering concerns, it is very easy for us to give up and call it quits. Well, if it is that *easy* to give up when you are unhappy and oppressed, just imagine what you can do when you are not.

Unfortunately, as much as we try ignoring those perplexing contemplations, they still do a nasty number on us, causing us to throw up our hands and walk away. These unfavorable reflections also cause us to think negatively of ourselves where there is little or no self-confidence. For some reason, when we are despondent it is impossible to feel good about ourselves so we run and hide. Those annulling emotions keep us entrapped by fear, subsequently, believing that nothing will ever change. Because negative thoughts build gradually over time, we struggle in silence while the whole world goes on about its business. Sadly, many of us remain in a "do-nothing" state of mind for what seems like forever, until someone finally comes along with the answer to our prayers. It is only then that we decide to make a change in our alarming situations.

Likewise, a lack of self-assurance contributes to mood swings, personal dissatisfaction, and in most instances, failure. Failure, causes our emotions to have a field day with us while we are moping around the house with our lips all poked out. Subsequently, our minds are busy playing tricks on us. Since we can easily surmise that a person with no hope believes that their future will be full of opposition, is there anything we can do to change this senseless way of thinking? I believe that there is.

If we can do anything to prevent someone from losing *hope,* showing that person appreciation would certainly be high on the list. "A person who feels appreciated will always do more than what's expected." It is the immediate rush of adrenaline that is felt when shown how much they truly matter. Similarly, people need to feel loved and appreciated to lessen those horrible feelings associated with hopelessness. Has there ever been a time when you felt like giving up or throwing in the towel? Most of us have felt that way at least once or twice—maybe even more than that.

There is a lot more we can do to rid those feelings of desperation than to add our names to the waiting list to see a therapist, *if* we are serious in terms of our health, wellness, and future. Sometimes, life hits us so hard that we lose that locus of control and everything around us goes haywire. For instance, we have been knocked to the ground and dared to get up, spit in the face because of our race, and hit in the head and left for dead. More than that, our husbands have lost their minds, our children are way out of line, and sometimes we do not even have a dime. This is where some of us find ourselves when it seems as though our world is upside down. As a result, the perplexities of hopelessness and despair are sending us to an early grave because we are afraid of changing the way we think.

Vaclav Havel, philosopher, and former President of Czechoslovakia said it this way: "Hope is not the connection that something will turn out well, but the certainty that something makes sense, regardless of how it turns out." As a woman who knows all too well what it feels like to lose hope, and has beaten the odds of ever regaining it, I invite you to become a partner with me in carrying out these simple, but edifying, acts of kindness. I wrote them with the intention of relieving some of the pressures doled out to us by life. Feeling hopeless is certainly one of those things that keep us weighted down.

I realize that most of us think of an act of kindness as a memorable deed that can make someone else's day brighter. You will also find that the simple things we do for ourselves is like honey to a bee. However, in order to kill two birds with one stone, I decided to put a little twist on how we can turn our own ill-fated situations around, while honoring others. I have learned that doing something good for someone else makes us happy on the inside even in cases where we get nothing in return. The happier we are, the better we feel about ourselves. Giving to others massages the heart.

Sometimes, it's the small things we do for others that leave a lasting impression when done out of genuine love and concern. So, you see, the size of the deed does not matter. That should not be our focus anyway right now, especially when we are hurting and desperately in need of a healing. There once was a time when people felt that materialistic items, such as fancy cars and expensive homes, would bring them happiness. When you visited their homes all you saw was a bunch of "stuff." No matter what you do, some people will always feel that the accumulation of things will define who they are. If they have three or four cars then must be somebody. If they have a lot of nice suits, they must be important. Well, I'm here to tell you that it's not that way at all.

Over the years, I somehow accumulated a lot of "stuff" that eventually piled up so high that I could barely see the closet floor. Did that make me important in the eyes of others? No it didn't. Did it make me happy? For a minute, it did, but after that—well, you know the rest of the story. It usually ends the same way for us all.

People experience true happiness when they do something nice for someone else. It helps to remove our personal needs out of the equation when we focus on something that is much bigger. Making someone else's day is definitely a huge, but rewarding undertaking. Consequently, if you really want to make a difference in your own life, give someone the gift of appreciation. Doing something unexpected can change *your* life for good.

"The Seven Acts of Kindness" that I am going to introduce to you will ultimately benefit both parties involved. Firstly, they will bring joy to the one who is doing the giving. Secondly, the individual on the receiving end will have an opportunity to receive an awesome gift that is totally unexpected. What more could one ask for? No matter what were the appalling circumstances that caused you to lose hope, these effortless gestures will perhaps rid many of those distorted insecurities, which are hidden on the inside of you. There is always something that can be done right now. Matthew 5:16 puts it this way: *"In the same way, let your light shine before others, that they may see your good deeds and glorify your Father in heaven"* (NIV).

I am hopeful that you will feel comfortable implementing at least *one*, if not *all*, of the kind gestures that I am suggesting. Since all of us experience challenges that might warrant an immediate resolution, "The Seven Acts of Kindness" will do the trick. Listen carefully as I explain what happens when we implement these surprisingly wonderful deeds. At the end of the day, they are what every woman needs. Let's take a peek.

Act of Kindness #1: *Remind yourself that you are getting better every day in every way. This kind gesture requires you to get out of your comfort zone and take action. It might feel awkward at first, but at the end of the day, you will value your potential. In order to reaffirm your realm of possibilities, try saying a few kind words to yourself and watch what happens. The more you say it, the more evident it will become—to everyone. Sometimes, the best gifts are the positive words that come out of our own mouths.*

For starters, I am not going to reinvent the wheel here by asking you to do something that you have never done before. Only people who talk the talk, but have never walked the walk, do things like that. Although I know this might sound a little strange to you at first, but I am going to ask you to talk to yourself every chance that you get from now own. When we hear ourselves speaking aloud, it brings our mind into agreement on that topic. If we are bold enough to say it, we should be bold enough to believe it. Faith moves us into action at this point. There is no turning back.

On the other hand, you know what they say about people like us who talk to ourselves. However, we are not going to worry our pretty little heads off by responding to those nonsensical accusations. Right now, there are more pressing concerns in front of us that demand our immediate attention. Therefore, you have my permission to encourage *yourself.* Sometimes we have to speak victory during the test. Go ahead and pat yourself on the back. If it requires you to yell at the top of your lungs, then by all means, do so. We are constantly talking to others or someone else is always in our ear, so why not? There is nothing like a good old fashion down to earth chat with ourselves to steer us in the right direction.

When we listen to our own voices, the solutions to our problems somehow seem more realistic and attainable. The remedy appears to be in reach instead of some place where it is nearly impossible to grasp. This indicates that we are on the right track. Most of us know what will work for us long before we hear it from someone else anyway. Talking to ourselves is nothing new. It just feels awkward. Many of us would admit that most things we are not used to doing are uncomfortable at first. After a while, it becomes second nature. We can do them with our eyes closed or standing on our heads.

As we remind ourselves that, "we are getting better every day" this also includes making positive changes to our health, finances, and even more importantly, our relationship with the Lord. How can we walk away from something as valuable as that? This small reminder also gives us *hope* for the future and a new outlook on life. It is okay to talk yourself into becoming a better you. I did it too. Some days this was how I made it through. So open up your mouth and start moving your lips. Even you will be surprised at how fantastic you really are once you get started. Speak louder. I can't hear y-o-u. Your words speak life into your present situation. Don't you want to wake up the amazing person that is on the inside? The world needs incredible people like you.

Act of Kindness #2: *Light a candle for every positive attribute you noticed about yourself lately and take a picture of this commemorative event. Frame it and wrap it up as a gift to yourself for that special occasion in the near future. For some of us that occasion is just around the corner. If not that, we can simply enjoy a day of pampering ourselves. We do not need a "special" day to do that. We are worth celebrating every day.*

Each of us has unique qualities that are noticeable when we are in the presence of others. Hopefully those distinctive characteristics will resonate in the minds of those we meet for a lifetime. Sadly, many of our special attributes go unnoticed by *us*, so we fail to use them favorably. I challenge you to identify all of the wonderful characteristics that make you stand out in a crowd. After you finish jotting them down celebrate with lots of candles. You will be a changed person when you discover the best is already on the inside of you. You may have to dig a little deeper, but it is there.

It used to be that candles were solely for emergencies, but that is not necessarily the case nowadays. Candles have many representations. People use candles for just about any occasion, such as birthdays, holidays, and other memorable events.

Today, you are going to do something that you seldom do. You are going to celebrate you. It may not be your birthday or you may not have even gotten a raise; however, you deserve a celebration that is fit for a queen.

When a candle is lit it captures the attention of everyone in the room and brings everything into prospective. Candles also add life to any party. Their flickering flames brighten each room from corner to corner creating a festive atmosphere that lingers on long after the celebration has ended. Not only that, but candles represent unity. They have a unique way of bringing together the minds of people who come together for a specific purpose. The occasion could be happy or sad. The fascinating thing about it is that everyone in attendance seems to be on one accord while the flames from the candles are dancing all over the place. What a beautiful sight. Actually, it is very moving when you are in the midst of it all.

It is safe to say that most of us rarely talk about our positive attributes. When we do, it seems as though we are boasting, but are we going to allow others to dictate what we say during our private conversations too? Instead of waiting for someone else to celebrate you for all the good you do, hold your own celebration. You will always have the memories to prove your worthiness. What is preventing you from lighting those candles right now? Let's *all* celebrate and have a good time. This one's for you baby.

Act of Kindness #3: *Write a letter to yourself expressing how pleased you are about the goals you have accomplished in the past six months. Be sure to mail it. Mark the date on your calendar for which the letter will arrive at your address and meet the mail carrier with a great big smile. We could all use little pat on the back right about now.*

Sometimes, all the mail carrier leaves in our mailboxes are bills, magazines, and junk. I bet you are nodding your head right now because your mailbox is full of junk as we speak. Wouldn't it be nice to receive a letter or two that brings joy to your heart and put some pep in your step? Well, that can certainly happen. As a matter of fact *you* can make it happen. The good thing about it is that when you open your mail, instead of having a frown on your face, you will be grinning from ear to ear while reading its' contents. You may even become tearful at such astonishing news.

Wouldn't it also be nice to reflect on how pleased you are for accomplishing those goals that took forever to set in motion? This time you will be whistling "Dixie" instead of singing the "Blues" due to bad news. This is the type of news we do not mind getting up off the couch to retrieve. Incidentally, has the mail carrier left something special in your mailbox today? Is it that soul-stirring letter you cannot wait to read? If it is not, take out a pen and some paper. You have work to do. We can begin your letter by saying, "Dear Successful Woman . . ."

Act of Kindness #4: *Put a dollar into a jar for all of the kind deeds you did last week in the community* *or at work and donate it to your favorite charity or animal shelter. Giving to others actually helps us to realize that our own personal situations are not as bad as they may seem. In fact, it validates one of our many purposes on earth when we are in a position to help others whose lives may be in worse shape.*

Those who know anything about me can tell you that I am gong ho on saving for the future. Parenthetically, we all should be putting a little something away for a rainy day. We know that it is coming probably sooner than later. However, we are going to focus our attention on how we can make life better for someone else, while also reaping great benefits. The Lord *never* blesses us to keep it to ourselves. What is the point of having fat pockets, but no one with whom to share our blessings?

In order for the best to come out of us, we have to give our best away to others, daily. It is a process. It does not come naturally so we have to work at it. You heard me right. Action speaks louder than words. Please keep in mind these words of caution from Mike Murdock, a dynamic speaker and founder of The Wisdom Center in Fort Worth, Texas, "We reap what we sow not necessarily where we sow." What Pastor Murdock means is that when we give to others, we are going to get *something* in return. That is a promise made to us by the Lord. However, it might not come back to us in the same manner or from the same individual who gave it. One of the reasons why we are often disappointed, is that we look for the same gesture in return, or money, which can be a huge turn off for those of us who have not matured in that area especially when we do not receive it.

Therefore, a dollar a day can go a long way when others are hurting and need a helping hand. It would also be a smart idea to put aside a dollar or two for ourselves while we are helping someone else. Before you know it, you will be searching for another jar. Cha-ching.

Act of Kindness #5: *Bake your favorite pie or cake and slice it equally into pieces representing the number of persons you shared a smile with at work this week. Hopefully, you'll have to bake more than one pie. Attach a note of gratitude to each slice as you share these homemade treats in memory of the good times you all had together. Watch their reactions. They will greatly appreciate your kindness.*

Most women enjoy showing off our baking skills, and rightfully so. We have a lot to be proud of when we can brown a cake on the bottom without burning it. Regrettably, some of us do not have that wonderful talent. Those of us who struggle in the kitchen play it safe by staying in our lanes. Some of us even run in the other direction when we do not want to cook so we avoid making a fool out of ourselves or making someone sick. My parents owned a home-style restaurant for years before they passed away. P&S was a very popular spot for those who enjoyed a variety of well-prepared meals. Mom and dad thought they were the "best" cooks in the world. I dared not say anything that was contrary to their belief if I wanted to eat. Fortunately, I did not have to because they were

What to do When You're Feeling Hopeless

operating in their God given gifts. They knew how to stay in their lanes.

Isn't it wonderful when we can share our baking talents and words of appreciation with others, without going out of our way? It will not cost us another dime to divvy up a piece of delicious homemade dessert with someone who has made our day with a smile. Mom and dad were right. Who needs all of those carbs anyway?

Act of Kindness # 6: *Use some of the most common attributes that represent your charming personality and create a song. Listen to your favorite instrumental while singing these attributes aloud in front of the mirror. Go ahead; grab that paper microphone. This can have a domino effect on what others around you, actually think about you, but have not had an opportunity to share.*

Each of us has a favorite songwriter that we admire for the delightful ways in which he (or she) makes us feel. Did you also know that there is a potential lyricist inside of you? Why not use your writing skills to help *you* feel better when you are not at your best. You do not have to rap or clap, but it is necessary that you do something uplifting that will bring joy to your heart. What better way of magnifying those awesome personality traits than to serenate yourself with the *truth* in front of the mirror. When you are feeling sad, start humming those refreshing tunes. I bet you will soon feel better before the day ends. Who knows how far this will go? You may even have a number one hit inside of you. Wouldn't that be grand?

Act of Kindness #7: *Invite a special friend over to watch your favorite movie with you. Point out the similarities between them and the heroic characters in the movie while snacking on a freshly made bag of hot buttered popcorn and a cold glass of ice tea. The thank you cards will never stop coming.*

Most movies have a hero (or heroine) in them which we can all relate to in some form or fashion. When that heroic character reminds us of a special friend; why not tell them? Inviting that special someone over for a movie and popcorn is a real treat. Watching your favorite movie together will bring back memories of how they were there for you through thick and thin. Isn't this one of the reasons they are your best friend? Offer him (or her) a bag of hot buttered popcorn while explaining how they remind you of a specific character in the movie. Watch, as you light up their world by returning the favor when they were there for you. Most times, we do not have to leave the comforts of our homes to enjoy the company of that special friend. We do not even have to pay to watch our favorite movies over and over again. When was the last time you invited someone over for laughs and a little appreciation? Tonight would be great.

Overall, there is something special about the number seven. In case you are wondering why I chose to spotlight seven acts of kindness in lieu of some other number, seven has great significance. We have learned over the years that there are seven continents, seven days in a week, and seven deadly sins. There are seven divisions in the *Bible,* God created the entire world in just seven days, and we worship the Lord on the Sabbath Day. Of course, there are many other reasons why the number seven is significant; including its spiritual connotation, which represents completion. I also chose the number seven in hopes that when you have finished implementing them all, your situation would have changed. You will be able to see just how special you are as a woman. You are one of a kind.

When we give of ourselves to others, it unleashes a part of us that was once trapped by insecurity, self-doubt, and fear; all of which can lead to disparity, inadequacy, and hopelessness. Moreover, when we do something special for someone else, or even for ourselves, it gives us the edge we need to rid those feelings of uncertainty and vulnerability.

It is my desire that you will embrace "The Seven Acts of Kindness" in order to make someone else feel worthwhile when all *hope* is gone. Remember, you will *not* be left out of the equation. Though they are simple, and do not require a lot of our time or energy to put into action they can change our lives immensely. We can all use a little spice in our lives when our failures have gotten the best of us. You are on a mission. *"And we know that all things work together for good to them that love God, to them who are the called according to his purpose"* (Rom. 8:28, KJV). It is amazing how we can turn our hopeless situations around with a little encouragement. If a little invigoration will make a world of difference in the lives of others, just think how our own lives will be positively impacted with a great deal of reassurance.

Exquisite Words of Wisdom

"Hope is being able to see that there is light despite all of the darkness."
Desmond Tutu

~QUESTION of the DAY~

It has been said that, "helping others is like medicine to the soul." With this in mind, what are some other kind deeds you could do for someone else that would ultimately bring healing to your own soul?

_____

_____

_____

Affirmation: I will strive to lighten the burdens of those who are hurting, and as a result, my own life will be enhanced, not only because of what I have done, but because of who I vow to become in the process.
My afterthoughts concerning this affirmation are as follows:

_____

_____

_____

~Goal Setting Exercise~

My goal for reaching out to others in their time of need is to

_____

_____

_____

My time-frame to accomplish this goal is

_____

_____

_____

Once I have accomplished this goal, I plan to

_____

_____

_____

_____

~Reflections to Remember~

You Gotta Believe

When doubt clouds our minds, negative energy gravitates towards us.

Faith works hand in hand with the ability to look past the now and grab hold of our future.

There is not a single person on earth who has the ability to believe on our behalf. He (or she) can only believe with us.

~CHAPTER FIVE~

You Gotta Believe

How believing against all odds automatically declares you a winner

Against all odds, I learned to believe in *me* when everyone else counted *me* out.
To live a life of quality and achievement you must first believe that you can. There is not a single successful person who does not believe in him or herself. Confidence is the common thread among those who believe they can make it. The only way that we are going to obtain what we want out of life is to be confident when going after it. Therefore, we must get rid of all self-imposed limitations if we are ever going to accomplish our dreams and visions. So, what is your excuse?

Do you often find yourself doubting your potential because *you* refuse to believe in *you*? Are you the one who's left behind when others are passing through? Aren't you tired of sitting around proclaiming what *you* will do? That was me a while ago, so I have news for you. I walked around with my head hanging down because one was there for me. Out of all the people I'd helped through the years; I wondered how could *that* be? They did not seem to care that I sat up all night before crying myself to sleep. Some of them were so mean and evil; they were happy to see me weep.

Many would not answer, when I called their phone; no doubt, they knew it was me. Instead of lending a helping hand, they pretended to be very busy. When they saw me coming, they turned their heads and looked the other way. Although I desperately needed them, they did not have much to say. My heart had been broken and torn apart, so I needed a brand new start. It really did not matter much to them; they did not have a heart. Though they knew my story had surfaced all over; they did not seem care. This is why I am warning you, SO PLEASE BEWARE.

When others pretend to care about you, please do not be fooled. You know the ones who sit back and watch just to see what you will do. The very ones I cared about did me the same way too. Although I heard their smart remarks, I had to keep my cool. They laughed and joked, even whispered and sighed; they did not feel my pain. For the life of me, I could not figure it out, what did they have to gain? Everyone seemed to have it together except little old me. So, I had to pull myself together for the whole wide world to see.

Have you ever been in a situation where you knew you had it in you to accomplish something great, but due to fear and uncertainty, you allowed someone else to talk you out of doing it? Who hasn't had that discouraging experience in the past? As a matter of fact, this is exactly how dreams are unfulfilled. We are stopped in the middle of our destiny when we allow others to cause us to change directions in midstream; then WHAM there goes all of our visions, ideas, and dreams.

Better yet, have you ever attended a special performance of any kind and you said to yourself, "I can do that." Well, my dear, I bet you could. I would not doubt it for a minute. Then tell me, why haven't you done it? We are so quick to brag about how great we are without having a lick of evidence to prove it. Somehow, we are good at that. Some of us even go as far as shouting it from the rooftop, but if we are that great of a mover and a shaker, can you p-l-e-a-s-e tell me why hasn't someone else noticed it?

One of the fundamental reasons why we are reluctant to step up and step out is that we *say* we want something spectacular to happen on our behalf, but most times, we do not even BELIEVE it ourselves. James 1:6 tells us exactly what we need to do in order to believe that we will achieve our desired outcomes. It reads like this, *"But when you ask, you must believe and not doubt, because the one who doubts is like a wave of the sea, blown and tossed by the wind"* (NIV). We spend countless hours trying to convince ourselves and others, that we can do just about anything, but when push comes to shove, we fail at that too. We think that just saying it will do it, but this is *not* how it works. Our belief in what we want to accomplish has to be so strong that we can actually taste it, touch it, and feel it. We can even eat, sleep, and breathe it, if we really want it badly enough.

Everyone has dreams and visions, or something in life that we desire to achieve. Dreams are a series of unplanned thoughts that run through our minds. Boy, do some of us dream big. Unfortunately, it is not about the size of the dream, but do you believe in the dream is what matters most. It is going to take a lot of persistence and jumping over a multitude of hurdles to accomplish our dreams. That is what "successful" people do. We also have to exercise our faith if we intend to make our dreams come true.

If you need a little refresher, *"Now faith is the substance of things hoped for, the evidence of things not seen"* (Heb. 11:1, NKJV). Exercising our faith simply means, "to believe that we can get what we want, even though it seems like a long time coming." I can tell you from experience that it takes more than just "talking a good talk." When it boils down to putting our faith into action, *something* must be done towards that end. There are no more casual conversations about our intentions. There has to be belief and expectation, along with guidance, dedication, and know-how. In other words, when we declare that we can do a thing, we have to immediately switch gears, fast forward, and get to stepping. Of course, we have to also fast and pray, which is a no brainer.

Additionally, we have to strategically plant one foot in front of the other, so that our dreams won't continue to be floating around somewhere out there in cyber space. What I mean by planting one foot in front of the other is that we must have a plan to help us map out which way we should go. We cannot be wishy-washy and expect to succeed, which is what tends to happen to most of us when we truly don't BELIEVE. This is why expectation plays such a critical role in our lives. It increases our faith and helps to build the confidence needed to accomplish those dreams, visions, and ideas that make us uniquely different from others.

What good is it to say that we want something or can do a thing, yet we really do not expect for it to happen? That's bizarre. Most people would think that we had a loose screw upstairs, if we were to continue operating in a manner such as that. Take it from a girl like me; there has to be some proof in the pudding.

Sometimes, we are caught up in what others say about us, so we tend to forget all about our purpose. We are actually blown away by what they say. Without question, we are easily distracted and lured off the beat and path of our dreams, when we fail to close our eyes and ears to negative talk and negative people. It happens to all of us when we listen to those who we *think* we can trust. If I had a nickel for every time that has happened to me, I would be a billionaire by now and so would you. Let's see how I can help motivate you to get in gear. After all, you do not want to be in same boat next year.

Are you aware that it is easy for us to lose sight of our dreams when we are scattered, preoccupied, and all over the place? Listening to others who mean well, but do not realize our potential is even more daunting. Sadly, we keep allowing others to bend our ears with that nonsense. When this happens, we forfeit our chances of ever moving forward.

There are times when we are right on the verge of launching that new idea that will take us to the next level, then here comes Miss or Mister Know-it-All, who manages to convince us that we do not have what it takes. Who are they to tell us that we do not have what it takes, when all they do is go around acting like sneaky slimy little snakes? Why do we keep letting this happen to us? Shouldn't we be putting up a BIG fuss?

Although we come close to taking that critical leap of faith, it's heart-wrenching to admit that most of us will never see the fruit of our labor. We continuously listen to the wrong voice, as though there is no other choice. Are you familiar with that old saying, "You already have in you what you will need to fulfill your dreams?" There is no way that you can convince me that you do not want to succeed. All it takes is inspiration, hard work, and the courage to BELIEVE.

Have you ever wondered why some people are successful in life while others are full of envy and strife? At the end of the day, we are *all* in need of identical resources for survival: food, clothing, and shelter, not to mention air and water, if you want to be more precise. We were *all* born with distinctive gifts and talents, which were designed to enhance our ability to get us a-n-y-w-h-e-r-e we want to go as we travel this competitive road called life. However, we must all stay focused and not look to the left or to the right.

So, what is it that causes others to consistently hit the home runs or land that leading role in a famous Broadway play? Have you really taken the time to figure out why it is always that way? If you have not, guess what; I am about to explain it now, so when we get through chatting about this, all you can say is "WOW!" There are no little hidden secrets or hocus pocus, my dear. If others told you differently, they are sadly mistaken, you hear? It is not about a silver spoon, as others may perceive. The reason behind their remarkable success is the courage to BELIEVE.

The world is full of "successful" people. Simply put, success is a state of mind when it is measured by those of us who are actually running in the race. Not only do we have to participate in the race, we must BELIEVE that we can win or at least make it to the finish line in one piece. Sometimes it seems as though it will take a lifetime of preparation, but once we have accomplished a particular goal, we feel as though we can conquer the world. We might as well face it; today's society has made life a competition rather than a place of comfort. Women are competing for that perfect man, while he's out somewhere holding another sister's hand. Men are competing for that special lady, but she's somewhere acting *real* crazy. We have got to get a grip on what matters most if we truly want to succeed. Life is not about the competition we engage in, but rather, those of us who dare to BELIEVE.

I have learned that in order for us to be successful women at home, at work, or in the community, we must first master three extremely important "truths" or "confidence builders" as they are sometimes called. These confidence builders were carefully devised to help us reach our destiny, as we all plan to do at some point. Though they are as simple as ABC, they can have a profound effect on our lives as women. Take a deep breath and get ready to absorb this wealth of information. It is guaranteed to get you going in the right direction.

You would think that most women today would find it easy to apply these confidence builders to their lives, but that can be a huge problem for us all. This is why we are discussing them now, so that we will not continue to fall. If we want to fulfill our dreams, we must completely understand these very important things, (1) we must know who we are, (2) where we are going, and (3) which road to travel, in order to get us to where we are trying to go. I realize that this is a mouth full for you so we are going to take it slow.

In order for you to understand the importance of getting to know who *you* really are, *you* must first get to know the real *you*. You may ask; how do I do that? To begin with, you have to find out your strengths and weaknesses or likes and dislikes. In addition to that, what makes you tick intellectually, socially, or even spiritually? These entities will help to define the *real* you. Spend some time alone and think outside the box. As I told you before, you create the box. One more thing; treat yourself to a weekend getaway, if you can. If not, turn your bedroom into a retreat and hang out there. Sprinkle some white rose petals on that beautiful pink satin sheet. Then, take out a bottle of sparkling raspberry tea and have yourself a cold drink. Turn on your favorite music and enjoy the entire day. Keep in mind what Burger King says and "have it your way." You are going to need some time for a breather. Now is better than never.

In the first place, you cannot rely on someone else's perceptions of you for you to believe in yourself, especially when they have no idea of what makes you the person you are. If someone asked you to tell them about yourself; would you be able to comply? By the way, what would you say? Some of us don't know who we are, so we look to others both near and far. To me, that is like pulling a description of who we are out of a glass cookie jar.

Have you ever been in a conversation with a person who had a difficult time saying anything good about him (or herself)? Most times, that individual will be reluctant to engage in a conversation that puts them in the spotlight. As a result, the discomfort becomes glaringly visible. Maybe you have been guilty of this, but have not been able to put your finger on the reason why? Could it be that you really do not know who you are, and since you do not know, you dare not entertain that question when asked? It happens all the time. However, this is one of those uncomfortable questions that you *must* learn how to discuss with confidence, so please be prepared.

Psalms 139:14 lets us know that, *"We are fearfully and wonderfully made."* This means that we are created for "GREATNESS." Yes, I said, "GREATNESS." Even that statement is difficult for some of us to believe. We are startled when we hear it, and petrified to believe it. It is as though someone is speaking a foreign language that is too difficult for us to understand. So, what do we do when we catch ourselves daydreaming about our future? We conveniently dismiss those thoughts. In reality, we are saying that we are completely satisfied with where we are right now.

Well, if you do not believe that greatness is in your reach, you will always be discouraged by the calamities that seem to pop up one behind the other. Since we have been accustomed to habitual skepticism for the majority of our lives, it has become a chore for most of us to believe that greatness is anywhere in our immediate future; hence we settle for mediocrity. Do you want to live your life like the average Joe Blow? Average gets us nowhere these days. We know that it is out there somewhere for us, but we take the easy way out; once again because of fear and doubt. I have been guilty of that too, but now it is my turn to help you.

Those negative vibes we often get from others seem to outweigh how we feel about ourselves. When everything said about us is a put down, subconsciously, we began focusing on our shortcomings. Most times, we tend to get ourselves worked up over nothing. We eventually start thinking "I cannot do anything right" or, perhaps, "that will never work out for me." I am a firm believer that the more you speak a thing into the atmosphere, the more you will begin to believe it. So start speaking "GREATNESS" into your life right now. It is not out of reach for those of us who believe.

Without us even realizing it, doubt and disbelief have a tendency to creep up on us and take up residence in our minds. These constraints are difficult to evict. They have us afraid of shifting our thought patterns in the direction of success even though we know that it is the right thing for us to do. Our dreams seem as though that they are tied to an anchor. Most of them appear to be buried in the sand at the bottom of an ocean when we fail to go after them. Can you imagine the difficulty of being bound by an anchor that is virtually impossible to unravel? Ultimately, it is up to us whether we are going to allow the paralysis of not knowing who we are to cause us to be restrained.

Genesis 1:27 puts it this way: "*So God created mankind in his own image, in the image of God he created them; male and female he created them*" (NIV). Since we know that the Lord has done great things for us and through us, we are also capable of doing great things. We are made in his likeness. DON'T YOU LOVE THE SOUND OF THAT? There were times that I have been in shock when I managed to accomplish things that I had my doubts about in the beginning. Upon completing those seemingly impossible projects, I ran around in circles giving Him the praise for what He did for me. This is another prime example of why we must believe.

Furthermore, John 14:12 validates our potential for success by saying; *"I tell you the truth, anyone who believes in me will do the same works I have done, and even greater works, because I am going to be with the Father"* (NLT). Can you imagine decreeing that a thing will happen and it does? What can something like *that* do for me or you? The potential that we have will take us very far. All we have to do is BELIEVE in who we are. Knowing who we are is only half the battle, but it doesn't stop there. If it did, that would be too easy and some of us would think that life is a piece of cake. We would be sadly mistaken.

You must also have a strategy that will help you to accomplish your goals. If you do not have any idea you will find yourself falling in numerous sink holes. Consequently, it is impossible to reach your destiny, if you do not know where you are going. That is like sticking a blind man behind the steering wheel of a Mercedes Benz. From the outside, he sure does look the part, but on the inside, he cannot see a thing because it is dark.

Some of us are in the dark when it comes to executing our plans for achieving our goals. We are apprehensive about going at it alone. As a result, we leave it for someone else to do. You cannot turn your life over to another person and expect for him (or her) to get you where you need to go. You must get in the driver's seat and head towards your destination. Certainly, there will be many bumps and bruises along the way; that's life. However, this is where our faith kicks in again. It is always there when we need it; we just have to use it. If we keep on pursuing our dreams, they are bound to come true. I can talk until I am blue in the face, but what are you going to do?

I believe that you finally understand how imperative it is to master the first two confidence builders. Now we are going to focus on how to get to the next level as we discuss the third entity that moves us forward. For that reason, I will be discussing the importance of shifting gears in the direction of your desired goal. Isn't it funny how our lives have to be mapped out as if we were going on a trip that is full of adventure? I guess that wouldn't be so bad if we only knew where we were headed.

Though we frequently use the GPS (Global Positioning System) for tracking our daily travels, there are still times when we get lost and need to find our way. We do this so that we will not end up some place other than where we were going. This scenario can also be applied to achieving our personal goals. It is imperative that we stay on the right path. Together, vision and purpose, act as a GPS tracking system for helping us reach our goals in life. Vision, is the ability to see or to perceive which direction we need to travel in order to accomplish our dreams. Purpose represents the reason why we want to fulfill those dreams. Vision and purpose go hand in hand. You know it is impossible to do anything without a concrete plan.

Proverbs 28:19 encourages us to have a vision regarding our future. It reminds us that, *"Where there is no vision, the people perish"* (NIV). Our mental GPS, which operates on vision and purpose, will steer us in the direction of our dreams. Although it may be difficult for us to keep moving in that direction, we have to avoid detours and roadblocks from all extremes. If by chance, the route that we are on do not take us to where we are trying to go, we can always change lanes and head in the opposite way. Delay does not mean denial. It only means that we have to wait in line a little longer. I have found that waiting on my dreams has definitely made me stronger.

There is no way around it we must know how to get to where we are going, even when the odds are against us. As women, there are many decisions that we have to make on top of our hectic schedules and industrious careers. At times, it seems as though we are lugging around the world on our shoulders although we are already in over our heads. I am surprised that some of us can even get an ounce of sleep at night. If we are not trying to wiggle our way out from underneath a rock, we are trying to help someone else to figure out the next move. That is how most of us live our lives. Our minds are usually some place other than on our own circumstances. I am not saying we shouldn't consider others, but when we are distracted, there is no telling where we are going to end up. Isn't that the way it is when we are driving on the road for real?

When we do not go down that road that lead us to success, our botched-up lives will still be in a terrible MESS. Once we truly understand the relevance of knowing who we are, where we are going, and which road we must travel to reach our destiny, we will be well on our way to understanding the power that lies within you and me. This is another wonderful reason why we gotta BELIEVE.

I can truly say that the confidence builders that I shared with you have enabled me to become a more purposeful Woman of God. More than that, they helped me to utilize many hidden talents that were waiting to be shared with women who are in need of direction. This is my purpose in serving Him. Sometimes, all we need is a kind word or for someone to tell us that they BELIEVE in us. After we hear it a time or two, there shouldn't be anything we can't do.

This scenario also reminds me of a new actor or singer who is anxiously waiting to be "discovered." It is not until the standing ovation and the curtain is drawn, or the sale of a million copies of that special CD that their true talents are magnified for the whole world to see. This is the way it is for us when we allow these "confidence builders" to work on our behalf. We finally realize that we really do have what it takes to remain on the winning team and to fulfill our dreams. Now do you understand why I say, "YOU GOTTA BELIEVE?"

Ladies, it does not hurt for us to be refreshed in the things that we probably already know, but have failed to implement in our daily lives. By doing so, it will motivate us to push past our pain and shortcomings, as we begin exploring and embracing those distinctive attributes that help shape our uniqueness as women. If you have already put these "confidence builders" to work on your behalf, then my hat is off to you. If you have not, I can help you to employ them in every situation that applies to you.

These "confidence builders" are as easy as ABC. They were distinctively designed to help women like you and me. The road that you travel might be quite different from the one that I am on, so keep on believing, my sister, before all *hope* is gone. "If you keep on believing in all that you say and do; those around you will start believing the same thing too."

Exquisite Words of Wisdom

"When you doubt your power, you give power to your doubt." Honore de Balzac

Here are five confidence builders you should say to yourself daily:

1. *I am capable of succeeding even in the face of danger.*
2. *There will always be trouble, but without it, I wouldn't be me.*
3. *Standing up for what I believe doesn't necessarily mean I'm wrong; it just means I'll have to keep standing until someone notices me.*
4. *When I don't know which way to go, I'll look up at the sky. Surely, a rainbow will appear and lead me in the right direction. All I have to do is follow.*
5. *At times, the light is incredibly dim, but who's more capable of flipping the switch than the one who's closest to it. Me.*

~QUESTION of the DAY~

Often times, when we run upon an unexpected roadblock in our lives, we immediately begin to doubt. When doubt or unbelief tries to discourage you, what will you do to circumvent those adverse feelings that are bound to come your way?

_____

_____

Affirmation: I believe in the power that resides inside of me.
My afterthoughts concerning this affirmation are as follows:

_____

_____

~Goal Setting Exercise~

My goal for increasing my faith is to

_____

My time-frame to accomplish this goal is

_____

Once I accomplish this goal, I plan to

_____

_____

~Reflections to Remember~

The Twenty-Four Hour Woman Syndrome

If you afraid to tell someone "no" you are setting them up for disappointment down the road when you can't meet their demands for sure.

Our own well-being is the first thing that gets neglected when we constantly try to appease others.

Busyness does not equate to effectiveness. It just means that some things are bound to be left undone.

~CHAPTER SIX~

The Twenty-Four Hour Woman Syndrome

Why it's okay to say "no" and mean it

Are you the kind of woman who just can't say "no"? What I am referring to is the inability to say "no," out of fear of hurting someone's feelings, or letting him (or her) down. Surely, you must know by now that some women have a problem with *that*. We often bite off more than we can chew and take on more than we can do. Sometimes, we just don't think before we leap. This is what gets us into *big* trouble with ourselves and others, when we continuously say "yes," although we really mean "no." Sounds like a case of double-mindedness to me, don't you agree?

For years, research has validated that women have a natural tendency for wanting to please. It's in our genes. We want to make everybody happy all the time. Grant it, we do a fantastic job at making wishes come true, but at what cost?

Instead of shifting the heavy load, some women would rather grin and bear the heartache of being used or dumped on, for the sake of making life easier for those we don't want to disappoint. Some of us have even gotten ourselves in a pickle when we've graciously agreed to lend a helping hand. Yet, we continue in that same vicious cycle anyway. Consequently, we had to learn the hard way that we were way in over our heads from the start.

Well, I have news for you. Usually, when someone asks us for a favor, we have been singled out. We are also the preferred choice. Nine times out of ten, it is no secret that we are not going to turn them down. Who in their right mind would ask for assistance assuming that the answer would be no way? Some of us have gone ahead and put our lives on hold to ensure someone else's happiness, but look where that has gotten us. As a result, our own lives have been conveniently placed on the back burner just longing for an opportunity to come our way.

We would rather "fake it until we make it" when it comes to disappointing our confidants, but who gets the bad end of a situation when we refuse to voice what is truly in our hearts? Why do we keep up that never-ending façade? This is what most of us do when we allow ourselves to get backed into a corner by not saying say no. Meanwhile, our plates are *running* over with the concerns of the world, while we are *running* all over town trying to appease our buddies. Consequently, we are *running* ourselves ragged.

When will we ever learn that it's okay to say no? I am appalled at the number of women who can't or won't. Something in our mind tells us that we are going to injure or perhaps lose that special friendship, if we don't do what we are asked. Is it *really* that important to maintain a relationship if our health is threatened, our finances are ruined, or our dreams are constantly being put on hold? If you think that it is, please think again. Once we realize that it's impossible to make everyone happy all the time, it will be much easier for us to be true to ourselves and them. I learned that, "the courage to say *no* will far exceed the fear of saying yes," primarily when we are unable to fulfill the overwhelming demands that are placed on us daily.

Sometimes, when we allow ourselves to get caught up in what others say or feel, nothing else matters at the time. What we learned through the years concerning harmony and stability has somehow gone out the window. Our health, personal relationships, and even our finances can take a serious hit when our lives are unbalanced. Quite often, we pretend that we can snap our fingers to make things happen, but in all honesty, when we get behind closed doors we are actually praying that no one will ever notice the pain that is practically killing us on the inside. Literally, we can make ourselves seriously ill by trying to accomplish what we grudgingly agreed to do in the first place.

If that's not enough to get us to realize that there is more to life than breaking our backs to pacify others, I don't know what it's going to take. Some women are working our fingers to the bone while taking care of everybody else's homes. How can we be supportive and accommodating if our own lives are topsy-turvy, bent out of shape, and full of distortions? If we are coerced into doing too many things at once, nothing really gets accomplished anyway.

Isn't it crazy how everyone can see what is happening to us, but us? Although we are reasonably intelligent, courageous, and headstrong women, we must get ourselves together before it is too late. If we don't, others will begin referring to us as looney tunes with loose screws, or someone who is easy to get over on. WE ARE BETTER THAN THAT. Do you really believe that it is humanly possible for us to give our best when we are worn to a frazzle, scattered brain, and all over the place? Get a hold of yourself. Settle down.

By the way, here's a bit of advice for the easy-going, meek, and mild woman who walks around the office all day long with the cares of the world hovering over her shoulders; if you're not careful of the amount of time you spend making someone else's dreams come true, *your* life will be completely consumed. In the end, *your* sweet dreams will be floating around in the sky like a hot air balloon. Can I get a witness? I've seen it happen time and time again. Now it's time for the charade to end.

Let's sit down and chat for a while. I challenge you to take a g-o-o-d look at yourself in the mirror. What do you see? Better yet who do you see? Think about it. Could this be you? Are you the woman I am referring to? Is this one of the reasons you are unorganized, financially strapped, and most times you look and feel like "sudden death?" Come on now; there is more to *you* than that and *you* know it. You can do much better than that. I BELIEVE IN YOU. I urge you to take a step back and assess the *entire* situation before you plunge in too deeply and later discover that it's way too much for you to handle. I have been there. It's not a pretty sight.

If this is not you, I am definitely headed down your street. What about not being able to say *no* because you automatically assume right off the bat that if *you* don't do it; it won't get done? Are you still holding on to that same old mentality that no one can get the job done, but you? That's not true. Or, could it be that you desperately want to feel needed by everyone around, so you jump at the first opportunity to save the day? Perhaps you would like to be recognized as the hometown hero? I realize these are all loaded questions, but they were intentionally designed to be both thought-provoking and eye-opening at the same time. They were also crafted to encourage you to "hurry up with the quickness" and get your priorities straight. Notice I said *"your"* priorities. This command is of great urgency.

In spite of all the chaos that is happening in your own life you still insist on going to bat for others, consequently, smothering your dreams. You will be better off in the long run if you simply learn to say "no" to the deterrents that tend to get in your way. I call them distractors. These distractors, no matter how great or small, can cause you to lose sight of what you were predestined to do or become. They can lure you off the beaten path in a split second, if you allow them to. For instance, have you ever met a person who was on the verge of completing his (or her) college degree, opening a popular business franchise, or in the middle of writing a number one selling book, and they just quit? You probably thought to yourself that they were crazy or something didn't you? I sure would have. Before we jump to any conclusions though, maybe they were bombarded with too many things going on at once, so they failed to prioritize. This would definitely explain their irrational behavior.

When we are on overload, interruptions can inadvertently steer our thought processes in another direction. We easily lose focus when we are wrapped up in our emotions. There are other hidden distractors that seem innocent at the time, but they too can wreak havoc in our lives. For instance, what about something as simple as taking a mini-vacation or even going out to dinner "on the spur of the moment?" Although it did not appear much of a struggle initially, as soon as the bills started rolling in, you had a change of heart. You knew you couldn't afford those outings from the start. What a strange predicament that puts you in. Now, where are all those people you called your friends?

Ultimately, our focus becomes as warped as rotten planks on the surface of a hard wood floor, when we have too much on us at once. Our bones squeak and muscles ache whenever there is too much on our plates. We are squished and squeezed and even aging overnight. You might not believe that it is true, but what a pitiful sight. Fine lines and wrinkles appear heavily on our faces. So, we bombard the medicine cabinet searching for creams to erase it. No wonder we scare ourselves half to death when we get up in the morning and look in the mirror.

Go ahead and admit it; we are not thinking straight when we can't say no. Our purpose in life, though unintentional, becomes secondary when we are overburdened. We become unsettled in our spirit and grossly overtaxed with things that can either wait or be accomplished by someone else. We're in such a hurry to do the wrong thing. Moreover, it's baffling when the majority of us don't know how to fix the disheartening situations that we're in. Realistically, some of us are afraid to fix it. We're even terrified of the backlash and heated confrontations that might emerge as a result. In the end, we're the ones who are left "hanging by a thread." Did you hear what I just said? Um, did I happen to strike a nerve there? If I did, mission accomplished.

Please hear me out. It is imperative that you cut loose some of those time-consuming obligations you've taken on recently to fill the voids in your life. I'm referring to those nerve-wrenching commitments that usually take up the majority of your time. Trust me; you don't want to end up regretting that you haven't experienced all that life has to offer. Truthfully, you're too busy being busy. You're as busy as a bee, but you still feel empty. Who wants to go through life like that? Once you decide that the time is right to let go of those non-essential committals, you will be able to breathe easier, and focus on *your* future. After all, you're not getting any younger; right?

Women were born nurturers. Therefore, our inclination to help others overcome their hurdles and hard knocks is second nature to us. We do it all the time, although sometimes it puts us in a terrible bind. For the most part, we get a kick out of helping others cross things off their "to do lists" yet, our own must be at least a mile long. I have never been able to figure this one out. When we go out on a limb to help others, it puts a HUGE smile on our faces that assures us of our self-worth. That's just the way it is. It has also been drilled in our heads that when we put others first, we're doing the right thing. Although our efforts are certainly commendable, could this be another reason why we automatically step up to the plate without first weighing in on the consequences? We have the wishes of others plastered all over our minds.

It seems as though we're always being summonsed to assist others. Have you noticed that lately? Yet, we end up with our foot in our mouths when we agree to do the impossible. Why is it impossible for us to juggle everything that comes at us all at once? It's inconceivable because we're already overworked and stressed out. Face it. Our obligations are preventing us from spending quality time with our families, loved ones, and more importantly, the Lord. There is absolutely nothing wrong with helping someone through their hard times. However, there must be balance between helping them out and having our own ducks in a row. We have to learn where to draw the line. If not, we will always be behind.

Sometimes, all we need is an extra push or a swift "kick in the butt" from someone who has our best interest at heart or who will help us pull it all together. This is how some of us manage to get our lives back in shape. Someone else has to lay it on the line for us. We need to hear the truth about our idiosyncrasies and downfalls, regardless of how it makes us feel. I know the truth hurts. I am also a firm believer that the truth heals. Which would you prefer, to face the truth about your daunting situation and be healed, or continue hurting by living a lie and pretending to be "Superwoman?" The choice is yours, so choose wisely.

There are more and more women experiencing severe health problems including, heart disease, obesity, diabetes, and depression because we have overextended ourselves to the max. In spite of numerous warnings signs from our fatigued and overworked bodies, many women tend to push the limits without thinking twice about our health. Popular research has validated that some women have also experienced gastrointestinal problems, Alzheimer's disease, and premature death due to overexertion. These are all severe medical issues that can basically happen to anyone who wears themselves thin.

You probably already know that too much stress can also cause heart attacks and strokes in both the young and old. The daily news inundates us with dreadful stories and highlights concerning how stress affects our lives. It is one of leading causes of death in both men and women. If you look around, you'll discover that many people are leaving this earth like flies, due to an abundance of stress. It seems as though we can't handle many of the situations we've gotten ourselves into. What's odd about it is that we are a glutton for punishment. Instead of letting go and fighting our way out, we "dig our heels in" deeper, causing even more harm. I bet if we were to take a look at some of our family members or close acquaintances, we would definitely find numerous health problem related to stress. Let's see what we need to do to prevent this from happening to us.

When we experience excessive pain and fatigue, no one should have to tell us that something out of the ordinary is going on with us. However, some of us try to dismiss those annoying warning signs. We grovel at the thought of bad news about our health, so we hold our breath while wishing that our problems would magically disappear. Ordinarily, it doesn't happen that way for most of us therefore, we must take action to circumvent the dilemmas we've encountered. This is one of the reasons why I asked you such pertinent questions early on. I do not want this to happen to you. Another reason for the inquiries was simply to get you to understand how we get ourselves bogged down and stressed out. We have to learn the art of saying no.

The Twenty-Four Hour Woman Syndrome

It's amazing how many people are afraid of saying "no." Can you imagine that I used to be one of them until I figured out that everyone seem to be getting their needs met, except me. I wonder how I managed to give the preposterous impression that I would answer to every "beck and call?" Right now, I can't even begin to imagine. Once I became entangled in the vicious cycle of trying to appease everyone, I simply failed to do anything about it. Disturbingly, I allowed the situation to go on too long without noticing how badly it affected my health, work, and practically everything I touched. Stress had me digging my own grave and I didn't even know it. What a miserable feeling to finally realize that my situation could have actually been avoided if I would have had the courage to say no. I can see why they say that," hindsight is 20/20."

It is no secret that everyone has a limit before reaching a breaking point. Some people will inevitably push us to that point. They know exactly what it takes to tick us off and get us going. Some even manage to push all the right buttons to get our juices flowing. Since we're transparent in our dealings, it's quite easy for others to figure out, that we will do just about anything to make someone's day. Subsequently, it is imperative that we are not seen a pushover, or one who is easily influenced. No one has the liberty to walk all over us because we're being nice. Not only is it irrational; it's also irritating. However, it is up to us to put a stop to it. One of the means to remedy this self-centered behavior is to say *no* and mean it. Initially, it was hard for me to avoid saying no, but after realizing that I couldn't do everything; it was certainly easier the next time around.

Unfortunately, our situation is not going to get any better until we take a stand. We have to stop dragging our feet. If we don't "straighten up and fly right" these are some of the pitfalls that are bound to happen to us when we allow our arms to be twisted. First of all our dreams and visions will continue to be under lock and key. Regrettably, the keys to our future will be in someone else's ignition, while our destiny is being controlled by him (or her). Meanwhile, someone other than us will have the power to jumpstart our lives. What's even more discouraging is that our emotions will be turned on and off to the tune of someone else. Don't you think that is way too much power for others to have over our lives? I was told that, when we give up control of our lives we have to "fight tooth and nail" to get it back. That sounds like an enormous amount of work to me.

In addition to those dreadful pitfalls, our lives will be in turmoil, as we continue to juggle the numerous undertakings that we have in front of us. Let's not forget that our minds will be in an endless state of confusion; somewhat similar to a whirlwind that's spinning out of control. It's sad to say, but we'll also be a nervous wreck as we continue looking over our shoulders from day to day. It will also appear as though we are incapable of making decisions on our own. Is *that* the type of woman you desire to become? If not, it's time to get back in the driver's seat and tell that laborious situation to scoot over.

Before you get too anxious and overly excited about taking your life back, there is something else that I want you to know so give me your ear. It's the simple things that we don't pay close attention to that will cause our lives to be cluttered. We have to get rid of the clutter. If it means getting rid of someone who is holding you hostage by all means, do so. They are not going to like it, but at least you won't be tied down either. This is why I need for you to be mindful of what I am saying to you. Let me put it to you this way; you must be willing to do the work, so that you will not get caught up into what I call, "The Twenty-Four Hour Woman Syndrome." I bet my last dollar that most women will experience this type of infirmity at some point. Once this illness is contracted it is easily detected by others. Needless to say, those of us who have this dreaded disorder often find ourselves in denial.

"The Twenty-Four Hour Woman Syndrome," is in a category of unhealthy conditions all by itself. One of the drawbacks is that it usually hangs around for a while. Some women have most likely run smack into its symptoms and didn't even know what it was that hit them head on. Like many other deadly diseases, the symptoms start out unnoticeable and gradually increase as it worsens. The side effects are obvious, and can even be as life-threatening as a poisonous parasite, barricaded inside of our minds. In the past, women's lives have gone haywire and completely out of control. This harmful disorder, is known to be contagious, so watch out. It can also make you lose sight of your most memorable dreams and the aftermath will cause your life to go floating down stream.

Moreover, "The Twenty-Four Hour Woman Syndrome" has had a profound effect on the way women think and behave. It also hinders productivity. Many women have become complacent and have settled for less. This crippling disease has the propensity to wreck families and other significant relationships. Flawless work ethics have also been ruined. If by chance, you begin to experience any of the warning signs or red flags as I did, seek help immediately. It's the only way you'll be able to escape the lingering side effects that come along with it. This type of ailment requires the attention of someone who knows exactly how to cure it, once and for all. THE LORD GOD ALMIGHTY is that great physician. He will help you through the recovery process and get you back up on your feet. He's the best man for the job.

Take it from me; once you've been afflicted with this disorder, it's nearly impossible to recuperate. You must be strong, persistent, and confident. How do I know this? I was once "the twenty-four-hour woman." I was always running around like a chicken with my head cut off in pursuit of solutions to other people's problems. I would do anything, for anyone, to avoid conflict or to out run confrontation. I did this even if it meant going against my better judgment. However, the thrill of making life easier for others subsided when I noticed that my own life was in shambles. I had to make some serious decisions in order to keep my sanity, but it worked.

Let's see if you can relate to some of the circumstances that caused me to wake up. I knew I had to make some radical changes soon. A few years ago, I finally admitted to myself that I wasn't truly satisfied with the way my life was going at the time. At first, I tried suppressing those somber thoughts by pretending that they were not there. The harder I tried, the more it became evident that I was not losing my mind, as some had previously speculated. I felt droopy and drab, sometimes spiritless. I know it sounds crazy, but it also felt as though I'd sneezed too hard and my insides had fallen out. I was cold, destitute, and empty. In other words, lifeless.

There were times when I purposefully tried to hide. Unfortunately, I couldn't hide from myself. Sometimes I didn't even feel like waking up or rolling out of bed. Have you ever felt as though the life had been sucked out of you? That's exactly how I felt. It appeared as though I'd stepped out of my own body into someone else's. My life had suddenly become theirs. Although I tried pinching myself to see if it was just another bad dream, sadly, it wasn't. Life was getting the best of me. Death was knocking even harder. Every time I'd look in the mirror, the person that I saw was creepy; not the person I was accustomed to seeing by a long shot.

Over the years, my parents taught me that I was the only one responsible for my happiness. If it was going to happen, I had to be the one to do it. Whenever anyone would see me, I made certain my radiant smile was on point, as our paths crossed. It seemed as though a permanent smile had been etched in the middle of my face, with traces of bright red lipstick that helped to define my gregarious personality. My head was in the clouds. However, my intentions were not to appear cocky or conceited in any way. I merely wanted to be pleasantly remembered for giving it my best shot, while desperately trying to keep it all together.

Grinning from ear to ear, my demeanor was such that you would have never known about that little dark secret that I tried concealing from everyone I encountered. This was my usual way of hiding the pain and discomfort from the world. My friends said that I was a "pro" at doing that. Since I did such a great job at hiding my feelings, no one really knew how overwhelmed I really was. However, one more mishap and it could have been all over for me. Death would have accomplished what it had set out to do.

Those who knew me, would proudly say that if they needed anything done of quality that exceeded their expectations they knew exactly who to call. Even though they ranted and raved about my talents and creativity, I took it as a compliment and went on about my business. There were even times when it crossed my mind that I was a "do girl." I could hardly catch my breath before someone asked me to do this or do that. Before you knew it, I had already agreed to take on the responsibility without asking a single question. How foolish was that? Just as I thought, they wanted to see how far I would go to make others accept me by doing favors for them that others wouldn't dare do. Now, are you beginning to see how "The Twenty-Four Hour Woman Syndrome" can make you act before think? I thought it should have been the other way around.

There is no doubt in my mind that this was exactly how I became known as, "the one who would always come through." Although I frowned upon the "do girl" image, it would not have done me any good to get upset over it. The truth was staring me right between the eyes. Like most women would do to keep from jeopardizing their reputation even further, I kept my mouth shut, and pretended that everything was okay. I felt that staying busy would actually fill the void that was missing in my life, but boy was I sadly mistaken. Things got even worse. This was another vicious sign of "The Twenty-Four Hour Woman Syndrome."

Somehow, in the midst of my troubles, I lost that inviting smile and enthusiastic personality that distinguished me from others in the neighborhood. There were days where I couldn't smile. Something on the inside didn't sit well with me at all. It was only by *grace* that I managed to survive the discontentment that polluted my mind. Instead of blowing my cover, I pretended to have it all together by keeping my cool. Otherwise, I would have acted like a fool.

The burdens that I carried could have eventually taken me out of this world if I had decided to just give up. You do know that stress can kill you, don't you? If I did not have the Lord on my side, I can almost guarantee that my life would have been over a long time ago. The added pressure of taking on more than I could handle nearly did me in. Everyone depended on me, although at times, I was in a fog and as tired as a dog. Whenever anything needed to be done, it was always, "Go ask her; she'll do it." They knew I took pride in all of my endeavors and one more favor would not have made a difference, so they thought. Anything that I wanted to accomplish was going to be done with excellence or not at all. This is how I live my life.

As I continued to look back over my life, I was reminded of a little guy named Mikie. Mikie did whatever he was asked, seemingly without hesitation. Everybody loved what he stood for. That's mainly why he was pegged. When no one else would sample the cereal for its great taste, they knew exactly who to call on to try it first. Mikie's willingness to appease eventually became a cynical trademark for him. Today, Mikie, is known all over the world for his ability to satisfy others and put a smile on their faces. However, I wasn't that lucky. My desire to brighten someone else's day eventually became one of my biggest nightmares that lasted way past midnight.

For years, it seemed as though I was also carrying around the weight of the world on my shoulders. According to my dad, "I had to dance on every set." That might sound odd coming from a loving parent, but my dad always had a way with words that seem to cut right down to the core. What he really meant, was that I wasn't satisfied, unless I was busy doing something no matter what it was. Dancing on every set also meant that I wanted to have a hand in everything that went on. Under those circumstances, I was exhausted as soon as I got out of bed in the morning, and was droopy, drowsy, and drained long before going to bed at night. Yet, I did not know how to say "no" and stick to my guns.

You can probably relate to the time when you wanted to say "no" to something intuitively, but somehow, the word "yes" flew out of your mouth instead. Not a very good feeling ugh? Unfortunately, we end up in the same place where we started, with our lips poked out, arms folded, and feelings hurt. This is a classic sign of "The Twenty-Four Hour Woman Syndrome."

Some of the commitments that I promised to fulfill lasted for months. With everything going on at once, my own life was in shambles. If the truth was told, I wanted to explode. Subsequently, I began suffering from anxiety and depression. The horrendously painful headaches were a bit much, but I was too proud to tell anyone. Sometimes I curled up in a knot on the floor and prayed that GOD would take the pain away. Isn't this what happens to a lot of us when we allow things to get out of control because we have an insatiable desire to please? We bring on illnesses that never should have happen to us. At the same time, we suffer needlessly when all we had to do was say no and mean it. How could I have ignored the apparent signs of "The Twenty-Four Woman Syndrome?" If they would have been a snake, they would have bit me.

When we allow ourselves to get into situations as such, we are at a disadvantage. Subsequently, our ambitions and desires are delayed. Our needs seem to be conveniently placed on the back burner just waiting to be resurrected. Have you ever wondered why it is so difficult for some women to step aside and allow someone else take up the slack? There could be a million and one reasons why this occurs. We could go on all day trying to figure it out and still come up empty handed. However, the only one who truly knows the answer to this question is that individual. If by chance you discover that you have contracted "The Twenty-Four Hour Woman Syndrome," do not be discourage; do something about it. You are equipped with everything you need to make that change today. Do not put it off any longer.

Now that you know there are two individuals routing for you to make those necessary changes in your life, the Lord and me, you can create a new beginning. YOU ARE IN CHARGE. If you don't remember anything else that I've said thus far, please remember this, "You were never created to be *all* things to *all* people *all* of the time." You were created by God, first and foremost, for His enjoyment of your humble service to Him, above that you give to *all* others. You were also created to carry out His Divine Will for your life. You can't go wrong there. I implore you to take a deep breath and take the heavy load off. Keep moving towards your destiny so that you can be totally healed of "The Twenty-Four Hour Woman Syndrome." You don't want to run yourself in the ground and people can certainly cause this to happen. My sister, YOU CAN DO THIS. No one wants to be thought of as "easy game." You cannot get to the next chapter of your life unless you turn the page.

Exquisite Words of Wisdom

"When you say "yes" to others, make sure you are not saying "no" to yourself." Paulo Coelho

Here are four easy ways to say "no" without feeling guilty:

1. *If someone asks you to do something without adequate notice, this is a great response; "I really do appreciate the fact that you trust my efficiency in getting the job done, but since this request demands immediate action, may I suggest that you ask . . ."*
2. *If someone asks you to do something that competes with the time you allotted for yourself, this is a great response; "I'm honored you've requested my assistance in this matter. It lets me know how much you value my resourcefulness. However, if you would have informed me a few weeks earlier, I certainly would have tried to be more accommodating at the time."*
3. *If someone wants to borrow money, but you really don't care to lend it, this is a great response; "I appreciate the fact that you recognize how cautious I am when handling money. I would really prefer giving it to you*

instead. However, at the moment, I am unable to provide you with such gift."

4. *If someone wants you to go somewhere with them, but you really don't like the destination, this is a great response; "I enjoy your company and would love to be an honored guest, but at a different establishment. Would you tell me why you chose that one?"*

~QUESTION of the DAY~

When it seems as though you're carrying around the weight of the world on your shoulders what do you do to calm the raging storms in your own life?

_____

_____

_____

Affirmation: Though the world around me tries to keep me down today I'm getting up with a smile instead of a frown.
My afterthoughts concerning this affirmation are as follows:

_____

_____

_____

~Goal Setting Exercise~

My goal for making time for myself is to

_____

_____

_____

My time frame to accomplish this goal is

_____

_____

_____

Once I have accomplished this goal, I plan to

_____

_____

_____

_____

_____

~Reflections to Remember~

Women and the Woes of Life

When pain knocks us down faith picks us up. Look around you are still standing.

Although we experience hurt, the pain that comes along as a result, can actually help someone else to conquer adversities.

If you stay stuck on what happened to you yesterday, tomorrow will only be a dream that is trapped inside the bubble of your imagination.

~CHAPTER SEVEN~
Women and the Woes of Life

What happens when we allow our feelings to get in the way

"WOE IS ME" we often say, when things around us don't go our way. Life keeps passing us right on by, while we're gazing up at the blue sky. What are you doing to make life better? Please STOP pretending that you're under the weather. Why are you lonesome, pitiful, and sad? You don't look like your girlfriends; you always seem mad. Why do you behave so differently from them? It couldn't be Larry; I thought you forgot all about him. Your friends are out and about having a good old time, while you're sitting at home still trying to unwind. You better do something fast honey, baby, sugar pie or the life you want to live will pass you right on by.

You should listen to these words of wisdom; they'll come in handy someday. Remember there is HOPE, no matter what others may say. You haven't been yourself for a very long time; it's apparent you feel defeated and you've been on my mind. Of course, there are many setbacks that all of us women go through, but hold your head up high my sister; I went through them too.

What could it have been that made your life go tumbling downhill? You must do something soon; don't just sit there and be still. So, let's take a little moment to discuss what concerns me most; you have got to pull it together, my dear and STOP acting like Casper the ghost. When it boils down to surviving all that life puts you through, regardless of what others might think; your future is totally up to you.

For the most part, some of us just don't get it. What will it take to finally realize that our brokenness won't disappear because we simply chose to ignore it? The other bad news is that turning our heads the other way only gives us a temporary fix. Brokenness can stem from a perpetual state of disappointment or feeling like a failure when things don't go as planned. Broken is how we feel when we've been crushed by grief, crippled by trauma, or sundered by divorce. Unfortunately, it doesn't matter in which direction the telescope is tilted, when we peer through its lens, our eyes are fixated on the same thing; a life that's unraveled and unassured.

There are many setbacks that women will have to face if we don't put on our boxing gloves and come out fighting. These days, you never know just how hard you'll have to swing until you get in the ring; then it's SHOW TIME. There's no turning back now. This time, we're not swinging at the air when confronting our obstacles, but on the count of three, we're taking a direct punch for the sole purpose of knocking them out, cold. We can't bulldoze our way out of a bad situation, nor can we close our eyes and wish our ill-fated circumstances away. If it was that effortless, common sense should have told us that wishful thinking, without a course of action, is a sure sign of defeat.

Initially, I was hesitant in divulging such arduous memories, but the more I thought about how my life had pretty much ended, the more I realized that I couldn't sit back and watch your misfortunes chip away at your life too. My intentions are not to add to your distress, but merely to awaken the powerful force that resides inside of you. I understand if you're panic-stricken or perplexed. Life happens. Let's face it; we have all been faint-hearted about something at some point. Nevertheless, we really don't know the magnitude of our strength until we've been violated by someone that seemed to have the upper hand. Not only was I shaken I was mortified. Then, the day came when I woke up as a new person. That's when I realized that I had also awakened the powerful force that resided in me, but why on earth did it take so long?

By and large, we have been blessed with the ability to do the miraculous, although at times, we certainly don't act like it. Honestly, we are capable of doing far more than we think. Actually, we have the capacity to change our negative circumstances at the drop of a hat, if we desire. Can you imagine how much better your life would be if you truly understood the potential that resides in you? We say we want to change, but are we willing to do whatever it takes, when we know in most cases it's going to take a lot? Some women will take a few steps in the right direction, but a vast majority of us will do nothing at all. This is our biggest mistake. We wait until it's almost too late.

E-V-E-R-Y-B-O-D-Y has something about them that can definitely stand a change, including me. There are no exceptions to the rule. Don't look so surprised honey, you do too. In our minds, we are too short, too tall, too skinny, or too fat. If not that we are broke, disgusted, and messy or all of the above. If you know that you have some unsightly obstructions in your life which are holding you back, why not get down to the business of becoming a better you? We must stand up to those unfavorable roadblocks that tend to make us passive or indifferent. They leave behind unwanted scars that some of us will have to contend with for a lifetime. You've got to want it badly enough though or else you'll always feel constrained.

You must also be willing to go to bat for what you desire. This juncture in our lives reminds me of an expectant mother in her first trimester of pregnancy. Out of nowhere, the mother-to-be craves a slice of warm buttered pecan pie with two scoops of French vanilla ice cream on top for breakfast. She also demands a peaches and cream honey bun with creamy spinach pudding for dinner. That sounds gross to us. Irrespective of her uncomfortable condition, the woman refuses to give up asking for those unusual and seemingly outrageous food choices, until she got her hands on them. It might not seem like much to us, but to her it means the world to get her hands on exactly what she wants. Perseverance is the name of the game. Keep it moving. It's going to take more than a few tears to change what has been going on with you for years. If you're ready to turn your life around; put your boxing gloves on. We have a rocky road ahead of us.

Would you do me a huge favor, please? Let's take off the mask first. Realistically, you could probably use a serious makeover, right? Aren't you ready to embrace the "new" you? You can become a new and improved woman of God that is fabulous, dynamic, and empowering all at once. When that happens, you'll certainly be declared a *winner*. The "new" you is ready to be unleashed. She's well overdue. Let's pull her out of that shell and see what she's actually made of. You'll be pleasantly surprised.

Here's something else to wrap your head around; it doesn't make a bit of sense to keep doing the same thing and getting the same damaging results. One of my co-workers once said, "Doing the same thing over and over was like being married to the same man twice." Although I still chuckle every time I think about it, I wasn't about to take those witty words for granted. On a more serious note, I can tell that you're still facing some of the same problems that were staring you in face a year ago. A year is extremely long for *anything* to sit in limbo. You're even looking and feeling the same as you did when we spoke last. That was well over two months ago. If you don't believe me, take a look at those old water-stained family portraits in the wooden photo album underneath your bed. You'll be shocked to see that you haven't changed much at all.

For starters, do you see any resemblance between the photos that were taken of you ten years ago and your physical appearance right now? Take a look at those hairstyles you wore back then. They are the same ones you've been sporting for decades. Also, before going to bed tonight, take time out to sort through some of those outdated clothing you have folded up on the top shelf of your closet. They are the same items that you swore you were going to be able to wear again someday; but has that happened? No, it hasn't. Oh yeah, you even said that you were going to become "physically fit" by exercising and eating healthier to boost your self-confidence, but when? I see that you're still procrastinating. Finally, I haven't seen you smile in a while; why not? Have you sat down lately and had a little pep talk with yourself? Sometimes, we have to encourage ourselves, you know. If you haven't, I invite you to do that r-e-a-l soon.

Have you ever wondered how some women can show a little tenderness when pampering themselves, but you can't seem to make it happen for you? Why not take time out of your busy schedule and do *something* to make yourself feel super special? There's nothing wrong with spending some much needed time and energy tidying up those areas that are starving for attention. Listen ladies, we don't have time to dilly dally around with this anymore. Let me share with you what happens when we're entrenched by the wicked "woes" of life, which invariably, can range from physical illness to insanity. There are a number of other mortifying events that can also be referred to as the "woes" of life. These undesirable adversities appear in all shapes, forms, and fashions. Consequently, we are all affected differently by them.

There was a point in my life where I felt like the president of the Angry Women's Club, an organization where women would come together to hash out their problems and frustrations. My situation was oppressive to say the least. In fact, I thought that I would be taking the easy way out by hashing out my setbacks with several of the women I knew. However, I kept getting angrier by the minute. It was extremely difficult for me to come to grips with almost losing everything, from personal possessions that had been passed down for generations, to my self-worth, which appeared to have little, if any, value at the time. Even more, the constant mental abuse was intolerable and way too much for me to talk about in this book. It would probably take me until dooms day to tell you my story.

Thank goodness, I vowed to let go of the anger and hatred that wouldn't stop eating away at me at first. Realistically, I had to make a conscientious effort to forget about the emotional abuse that occurred almost daily to keep from losing it. Can you imagine someone constantly breathing down your back and making false accusations about things you never said or did, until it almost seemed like you actually did them? Surely, one of us was close to being insane and it certainly wasn't me. How do you ever get through something so evil? Better yet, how does anyone get away with such hideous intentions?

Perhaps, it was easy for others to say, "Let it go" but the erratic behavior shown towards me was too much. I fought like never before to overcome the ill feelings that were harboring inside of me. However, it took much longer than anticipated to change my uncomfortable way of thinking. Of course, the Lord was there to guide me through my hardships and battles; it just didn't feel like it at the time. The only thing I felt was unsurpassable pain. It was transparent that I could do nothing without the Lord's unerring guidance. This is when I decided that I needed to spend more time communicating with the Lord. I could not afford to miss a word that He said. When He spoke, I made it a point to listen. Spending quality time alone with Him enabled me to learn his voice. John 10:5 says it this way; *"My sheep hear my voice, and I know them and they follow me"* (NIV). Through the years, I learned that He never yells.

During the wee hours of the night when I felt the Lord's presence, I can recall sitting straight up in my bed, anxiously waiting for Him to speak. I was accustomed to our midnight chats and was very emphatic about developing my personal relationship with Him. The more we spoke; the stronger I became. Our conversations also enabled me to realize that He alone could change my perilous situation, if I put my trust in Him. I can truly say that when the Lord gets involved our problems will be resolved. There's nothing like His tender touch. This is another reason why I love Him so much.

After sincerely praying and spending time with the Lord, I got a new attitude; sort of like the one that musical artist, Patty LaBelle, sings about with an unprecedented voice that's in a class all by itself. Initially, the carnal side of me wanted to stay angry at the world for allowing my heart to be crushed, but it wasn't the world's fault at all. My misfortunes had nothing to do with the people on the outside, but rather, those who resided under the same roof. On a scale of one to ten, with one being the lowest, my self-esteem plummeted down the scale to a number one rating as a result. It appeared as though someone intentionally yanked my heart out, threw it on the floor, and smashed one of its valves to smithereens. Can you imagine how crummy life must have been for me at the time? It was p-r-e-t-t-y darn bad. You must have known that I was petrified, pitiful, and sad. The "woes" of life kept getting the very best of me so I worked even harder so I could finally be free.

As time went on, I was swept off my feet as vicious lies about my marriage were blown out of proportion by my haters who enjoyed celebrating my calamities. However, I still could not figure out why me. If I had a crystal ball, I would certainly use it to help ease the pain. For the longest time, depression and grief got the best of me as I walked around town with my head hanging down while contemplating what might come next. If it wasn't for my faith, I would have surrendered to the adversary that plotted my demise.

One sunny afternoon at about four o'clock, I headed to the grocery store for a few items that I forgot to pick up when I was there last. What a HORRIBLE day at work it was for all of us who were there. If anything could go wrong that day, it did. As I approached the front of the store, I must have been looking a mess because just as I step foot inside the door, my best friend Cookie yelled, "Girl, hold your head up high and don't let people see you looking like that!" I immediately stood at attention. From the tone of her authoritarian voice, I should have stayed in bed all day.

On my way to the condiments aisle Cookie reached out and hugged my neck so tightly that my eyes rolled to the back of my head. I nearly passed out in the middle of the floor. By the time she turned me loose, I almost wish I had. This was her usual way of showing how much she cared for those of us who were embarrassed by our afflictions. GOD had truly sent an angel my way on the day that I was about call it quits.

Cookie always had a way of getting my attention. One of her favorite things to do was to share some uplifting words of encouragement with anyone she just so happen to run into. Most times, I didn't know exactly what to expect when I saw her coming, but I know one thing for sure, she was going to tell it like it is. Her stern, hoarse, and forceful voice was as loud as a lion's roar and just as powerful. Cookie was also known in the community for her unselfish mannerisms. Everyone knew that she would give her last dime without even thinking twice.

Cookie had a habit of grabbing your hands and praying on the spot. She would then turn right around and give you anything she's got. The world could certainly use more people like her. I am grateful for the love and kindness she extended to me during some of the darkest days of my life. Her astonishing words of encouragement will forever linger in my mind.

Over the years, I had to learn how to "let go" and "let God" even though no one knew how wet my pillow was from crying myself to sleep at night. Because I applied the Word of God to my life, I am now playing a whole new ball game on a brand new team. It doesn't get any better than that.

Let me tell you about a time when I was stuck in a rut and didn't know exactly what to do. While dining out at one of my favorite restaurants I always seem to learn something new. For as long as I can remember, I was the inquisitive one in the family. My sister said I was "nosy." I didn't see it that way nor was I insulted by her remarks. I merely enjoyed the hot and juicy conversations that eventually turned into counseling sessions, as I feasted on the meal that brought joy to my taste buds; steamed broccoli, grilled salmon, and rice pilaf. My mouth is watering as we speak. Subsequently, as I listened to bits and pieces of those intriguing conversations, I was well-educated, in valuable life lessons that could prove to be beneficial later on down the road.

Across the aisle at the restaurant, a small group of women were mumbling and grumbling about their weary lives, so I swore I would not be like them. However, I continued to get an earful anyway. At times, they laughed, cracked a few jokes, and even shed a few tears. Somewhere in the middle of the laughter, the focus of their casual conversations soon shifted. Somehow, their adversities became the center of attention. A subtle change in their tone of voices clued me in on the seriousness of their heated discussion.

Without giving it a second thought, I did exactly what most "nosy" people would do. I slowly scooted over to the edge of my seat where I sat next to the stained-glass window and gradually tilted my head to the left, as I cocked my ears in their direction. In order for me to make out what the women were saying, I paused and listened intensely, while holding my breath. Finally, I slowly exhaled before my face turned black and blue. This would have definitely exposed my intentions. With my heart pounding fiercely, and my tiny ears burning like fire, I reached for my glass of ice tea, hoping it would help relieve the tension that consumed my entire body.

By now, there were tears streaming down the faces of the entire crew. Everyone appeared to be memorized by the buzz floating around the reserved table. One of the women who candidly expressed her concerns about her deteriorating marriage nearly brought tears to my eyes. I mean it was a real doozy. After all, at one time in my life, I was nothing but a "bag of water" according to my oldest brother Randy. Of course, I didn't want to look like a fool nor appear to be eavesdropping; therefore, I quietly slid my bottom right back in the middle of my seat and started chopping away at my food, as though I had been sitting there all the time. The good thing about the entire ordeal was that I had learned what *not* to do when facing similar adversities from the women who seemed to be in distress.

From what I could gather, the women at the restaurant were struggling with co-dependency, loneliness, and low self-esteem. The other matters of contention were insecurity, educational restraints, and career setbacks; all of which contributes to the "woes" of life. These bothersome situations are prone to barricade our progress. The "woes" of life can also incarcerate our dreams and stifle our visions. No doubt, they can lead to non-productivity and complacency. At least one thing's for sure; it doesn't have to be that way forever.

Although women are strong and courageous human beings, the feminine side of us enjoys getting attention from someone of the opposite sex. Oh, yes we do. I'm sure you know how it feels when you're all dolled up from head to toe in your tailor-made suit, high-heel stilettos, and matching purse. Let's not forget about the luxurious three-piece jewelry set that made you feel like a million bucks when it sparkled. Those who saw you thought you had just stepped out of a glamour magazine. Nothing was out of place. Then, all of a sudden, a tall, sharp, and outrageously handsome man mysteriously appeared out of nowhere and winked his eye at you.

After getting over the initial shock chills ran up and down your spine, the microscopic hairs on your arms stood straight up, and itty-bitty butterflies danced around in your stomach for more than an hour. I bet you forgot all about your troubles at the time. Am I right about it? Grant it, we are reasonably intelligent, super-successful, and beautiful women from the inside out. More than that, we are God-fearing, caring, and powerful women. Though we are blessed with these wonderful attributes, the atrocious "woes" of life always seem to stand in our way. The good news is that once our troubles have been exposed, we *can* do something about them. We don't have to run and hide anymore. No more shame. Stay with me a little longer while I share with you some of the drawbacks of these overwhelming concerns.

Co-dependency is one of the vicious "woes" of life that can be a huge problem for both men and women alike. Basically, co-dependency is a state of mind that has a lasting effect on any relationship where there is one person who has to be in control at all times. Co-dependent relationships are one-sided, destructive, and in most instances, abusive. The dominating partner thrives on being in charge. If he (or she) does not get their way, you will have HELL on your hands and they don't even care. They're mainly concerned about themselves even in the threat of danger. You will most likely be on your own. I was once married to a man just like that. No matter what, Dale wasn't satisfied unless things were going his way. It was his way or the highway, as he would say.

What a shame it was that Dale couldn't enjoy life without always having to be in the driver's seat. Some people are just that way. It makes them feel superior when they think they have their foot on your neck. It was as though I didn't have a say in the relationship at all. I felt like I was in prison; waiting for my day to escape. I was afraid to say what was on my mind because if it didn't sit well with him, of course I would never hear the end of it. What is a relationship without freedom of speech? Moreover, what's the point in speaking when no one listens? Most of the time, I had to "walk on egg shells" throughout the marriage, but little did he know; I was walking and praying for my release from him at the same time. When things got too hot and heavy I was able to escape to freedom and start anew, without looking back. You never know the trap you're in until you've experienced what's outside of the cage. Freedom awaits us all.

Conversely, the non-controlling, usually female partner in a co-dependent relationship feels the need to be controlled. She often thinks of her male partner as being more important. Her lack of self-confidence, contributes to feelings of inadequacy and failure, even though she is quite capable of fending for herself. Unfortunately, she is afraid to make a move. Of course, we can all identify both women and men whose paths we've crossed that decided to stay in this type of unhealthy relationship. Somewhere down the line, they have been lead to believe that they cannot make it on their own. However, the truth is, they never really tried.

Thank goodness, this was not the case for me, but the women in the restaurant sure did have a problem with co-dependency. I overheard one of the women say, "I don't know what I would do if my husband was to leave me." On the contrary, if we only knew the detriment we cause ourselves when we speak such morbid words over our lives, we would certainly reframe from saying them. Surely, we must have *some* idea. We're just accustomed to thinking the worst before it ever happens. Most likely, we will cry for a few days, hide from our friends and loved ones, and eventually brush ourselves off in preparation of starting our lives all over again. That's what I did. Some of us might even break out in a song and dance to prove that we can make it on our own. This is how we have survived for decades. It is not about to change now.

Unfortunately, the statement made by the flustered woman is all too common. I believe I've even said it at least once. It was obvious she was agitated by her skittish behavior. The coffee cup sitting in front of her nearly slid off the table when she leaned forward to speak. Her high-pitched voice squeaked and squealed so loudly that it startled the waiter who was taking orders two tables away. I truly felt sorry for the woman, but I couldn't give her any advice. I wasn't supposed to be listening in on their conversation anyway, so I was between a rock and a hard place.

This is why it is critical that we develop and cultivate a personal relationship with the Lord. He sticks closer than a brother or sometimes even a sister. When we feel that others are more valuable, the Lord quickly reminds us that He has no respect of persons. We are all precious in His sight. He loves us just the same. If we can grab hold of this and get it in our heads; we will be able to bounce back from some of the most devastating experiences we've come up against.

Additionally, there is usually one person in the co-dependent relationship that is all for him (or herself). No one else seems to matter. If you discover that your partner only has his (or her) interest at heart, ninety-nine percent of the time, you are in t-r-o-u-b-l-e. Your relationship is bound to be one-sided, off-track, and out of control unless your partner is willing to change. It's no fun being in a relationship like that. By the same token, it's painful and pathetic. Once an individual is set in his (or her) ways, it's like pulling teeth getting them to see things differently. Eventually, the relationship will be destroyed because the self-centered individual is solely focusing on his (or her) own personal needs, while the needs of that person's partner remains unfilled.

Co-dependency can also prevent individuals from reaching their desired goals. As in any relationship, there is plenty of room for personal growth for both parties involved. When we're suffering from co-dependency we remain out of touch with ourselves and the world at large. Therefore, it becomes nearly impossible for us to function without our partner's approval. At times, it makes me wonder if we can think for ourselves. We work our fingers to the bone to conform to our partner's wishes, but we have somehow forgotten about our own goals and future ambitions.

Do you remember when you were once on fire about your dreams and visions? Absolutely nothing could stand in your way. You spoke very highly and confidently of your aspirations, but now all of that has changed. Perhaps you even managed to convince everyone who would listen that your dreams were going to come true and theirs could too. All of a sudden, you find yourself daydreaming about what could have been. Your mind is always some other place. Do you ever sit and wonder how could that have happened? Surely, you must know that it didn't occur overnight.

Some women would prefer playing it safe by remaining in a co-dependent relationship. Disturbingly, they have allowed their co-dependent relationship to become a safety net for survival, wherein, it was actually a bottomless pit from the beginning. Consequently, many women have become out of touch with themselves in the midst of falling for a man. What a waste of our time, energy, and talents. Ladies, we must think more highly of ourselves or we will continue operating in this same trajectory year after year. When we know better there are no excuses. It is high time for us to put those lame excuses in a bag and bury them. Let's say good-bye to our cop-outs and hello to great expectations.

Women and the Woes of Life

When I was younger, I can recall there being a well-known minister, probably in his early fifties at the time, who started off his Sunday morning television broadcast with these encouraging words: "Something good is going to happen to you this very day." Just the sound of those intriguing words moved me to change my iffy way of thinking about my future. Whenever the announcer introduced the ministry's broadcast, a warm and lasting sensation flowed through my mind, which confirmed that something GOOD was definitely going to happen to me on that day. My job was to expect it. Expectations is what's missing from *our* lives.

It's imperative that we live with expectancy. I believe when we have expectations, it builds our confidence and increases our faith in the Lord when our desires are manifested. Parenthetically, if we do not expect anything out of life, that's exactly what we'll get. How can we live our lives to the fullest without looking forward to something? Even a child expects a piece of candy or gum from his (or her) parents when they come home from the grocery store. So, why don't we have this same type of anticipation regarding our aspirations? This may be hard to digest, but we block our own blessings when we fail to make previsions to receive them. Let's use a simple scenario, such as purchasing groceries from the local food market to help us understand why some of us are still in the shape we're in. Here's what happened to my best friend Sara.

After choosing the items that would make her meals finger licking good, Sara, quickly dashed to the crowded checkout lanes with her red scarf swinging from her left shoulder. Nearly running over everybody in sight with her shopping cart, even cutting in front of those who got in her way, Sara refused to look back. She hurriedly made her way to the front of the checkout lane and began unloading the groceries onto the congested conveyor belt. When the cashier informed Sara that her purchase was fifty dollars, she carefully thumbed through her Gucci wallet and pulled out a hundred dollar bill, which she handed over to the courteous cashier as if it meant nothing at all to spend that type of money. It was obvious that Sara did not expect to receive anything from the cashier because she sprinted out to her car without ever thinking twice. When the cashier and several other customers tried getting her attention, it seemed as though she pushed the cart even faster while dashing out the door.

While loading the heavy groceries into the neatly organized car, Sara was as happy as could be. Her only concern at the time was getting home to her loving family. Throughout the week, Sara made no bones about not getting any change back from her purchase at the grocery store. Oddly, she continued her weekly routine as though nothing ever happened. Since Sara didn't expect anything in return, that's exactly what she got. Now, I would have had a problem with that. However, Sara went on with her normal routine as though nothing ever occurred. She didn't even contact the store manager to retrieve what was rightfully hers. This is what usually happens when we do nothing to foster our dreams. We don't believe that they will come true, or more precisely, we don't expect for them to come true. Guess what happens as a result? They don't.

We have to live with expectancy even though we've been accustomed to settling for less or nothing at all. We don't expect for good things to happen to us, therefore we operate in doubt. Doubt lends itself to fear and discontentment when we don't get what is rightfully ours. I know this way of thinking might sound foreign to you, but what I'm telling you is the best thing since apple pie. As time goes on, it is my prayer that women all over will wake up and "smell the coffee" soon, to prevent the "woes" of life from haunting us for the rest of our lives. Many women I counseled over the years seem to be well on their way. I want you to follow suit.

Moreover, if you had an opportunity to listen to some of the conversations women have with their close friends, you've probably drawn the same conclusion; we have a hard time coming to grips with low self-esteem issues as well. Some of us are better off at hiding it though. You will never know it exists, until you began to put it altogether. Most of the red flags are glaringly visible, but we keep them under wraps as much as possible. You'll probably be astonished to learn that low self-esteem can cause even the best of us to feel inferior. None of us are excluded.

Another constructive life lesson that I grasped from my parents was that "no one can make you feel badly about yourself." You have to allow their demeaning words to have a negative impact on you. Even so, you have to literally accept what they say as the truth. Now tell me, who does that? Surprisingly, some women believe *anything* that anyone says about them, particularly when it diminishes their character. One of the reasons has to do with having low self-esteem. Sadly, there is no immediate cure. A person with low self-esteem has to experience gradual periods of successful outcomes, in order to circumvent feelings associated with self-doubt. Once this happens, depression and doubtfulness will subside, whereas, their "can do" mentality will be reinvigorated.

I also had to brush up on what it meant by "anything permitted increases." This essentially means that, if we allow ourselves to be constantly put down by others, without stopping it, the ridicule will only get worse. Some of the words that come out of our mouths are infectious and unhealthy. It puts you in the mind of swallowing poisonous medicine. The more we stand for those debilitating words to enter our mind; our body entire body is easily affected. With that in mind, it is imperative that we don't let what others say about us get next to us. I know it's hard, but not impossible. You shouldn't bother listening to what others will say when all they want to do is stand in your way. Why don't you tell them to please step aside? Deep down within you're just glad to be alive. Hold your head up; stop looking down. Let them see you smile instead of wearing a frown. You are so beautiful; sis you really beam. Never let anyone cause *you* to have low self-esteem.

Additionally, low self-esteem can be caused by inadequate social skills, fear of being alone, and rejection. These are a few of the most popular reasons women experience this distasteful emotion. More than that, feeling unloved, unattractive, or unproductive certainly contributes to feelings of worthlessness. Now, are you beginning to understand why having the Lord in your life makes all the world of a difference?

When we face rejection or feel unloved, He whispers softly in our ears, that He loves us unconditionally. There is absolutely nothing we can do for Him to stop loving us. This should be music to our ears. By the way, He loved us first. Others may say they love us, but it usually comes with a hefty price. God has already proven His love for us by allowing His one and only son, JESUS CHRIST, to die for us. That's *real* love. As you experience feelings of low self-esteem, there is always something you can do to uplift your spirit, *"Cast your cares on Him; for He cares for you"* (I Peter 5:7, NIV).

Loneliness can also cause us to doubt our self-worth as women. Why is it that we can't stand to be alone? It always seems as though we are missing out on something when we're by ourselves, but are we *really* missing out? From the looks of it, everybody is enjoying life, except for us. Our friends are dating, engaged, or about to be married. They have healthy families and travel first class all over the world. Most appear happy and content, but don't be fooled. The optimal word here is "appear." If our friends were truthful about it, they would more than likely tell us that, "it's not what it seems." Subsequently, we can stop beating ourselves up, since we know for sure that loneliness is not a permanent situation; it can be reversed. Aren't you glad it's solely up to you to change your situation? Since you have the power to do so, why not be bold and daring every once and awhile. Do something out of the ordinary. It seems as though you're always doing something for others.

Isn't it about time you thought about you? May I make a suggestion, please? What about saving your spare change for a couple of months to treat yourself to a bed and breakfast outing or even a day at the spa? Afterwards, why not take a walk on the beach and watch the sunset while spending quality time with the Lord? Sounds like a winner, doesn't it? Try it; you'll like it. If nothing else, it takes your mind off being lonely.

Loneliness is also a state of mind. There is no single explanation for why people feel lonely. Loneliness can be caused by a plethora of issues including the death of a loved one, separation or divorce, and the lack of physical interaction with others. Furthermore, loneliness can result from being away from family and friends, relocating to a place where you don't know anyone, or feeling empty on the inside. When we think we're experiencing loneliness, we automatically try replacing those feelings of discomfort with people, objects, or situations that will hopefully reverse our undesirable way of feeling. Intuition tells us that we're not experiencing what "normal" people experience when they're in high spirits; therefore, something is missing. All we know is that something inside of us doesn't feel right when we are not connected, so we must be lonely.

Women can experience loneliness at various stages of their lives for a number of reasons, but let's set the record straight right first. An individual doesn't have to be physically alone to experience loneliness. Personally, I know of individuals who have been married or living together for years, yet they are still lonely. If you don't believe me, read between the lines when they spill their guts about a situation they're dissatisfied with. They'll even admit that they sit on the same couch next to their partners every day, and sleep next to each other in the same bed every night. According to some, the loneliness is still there. In all honesty, they are only occupying space in each other's lives.

I have found that people will always be lonely if they refuse to focus on the REAL reason behind their loneliness. Instead, they will continue wallowing in their pity. I don't know of anyone who wants to remain lonely for the rest of his (or her) life, do you? So, let's explore what can happen as a result. Prayerfully, if you are feeling lonely, you will know exactly what it will take to reverse that damaging feeling.

I just so happen to be one who was married, yet lonely most times. No one had to tell me that something was missing from the one-sided relationship. Silly old me, was too afraid to do anything about it. The dreaded idea of facing life alone was even more alarming. I didn't have the guts to take advantage of the advice given to me by those who had already weathered the storm. Therefore, I had to contend with the freakish façade of pretending that my life was in tip-top shape, by smiling and waving at everybody in sight to circumvent the real deal. This went on for years.

The relationship was parallel to living on a deserted island with no one else around for miles. That's how lonely I felt. There was very little communication, very little understanding, no *real* love. What's a girl to do in a case like that? By the inquisitive look on your face, I know exactly what you are thinking, so I'll beat you to the punch: "Why in the heck did she stay married for that length of time if she was that lonely?" That's a fair question to ask. Sometimes I ask myself the same thing and I keep coming up with the same answer. Are you ready for this? I was scared to death of living on my own, not to mention my self-esteem was shot.

Everything I struggled for appeared to have been snatch away from me in an instance. I also felt that it was better for me to remain active in the community, or to immerse myself in the affairs of my tutorial business, rather than take a stab at life on my own. I literally became ill contemplating the "what ifs." "What was so difficult about that?" you may be wondering. The problem was that I should have been equipped to handle being alone. Instead, I depended on someone else to fill that empty space. How ridiculous was that? I couldn't bring myself to stop thinking about who was going to help me rise above the pain and embarrassment of starting my life all over again, which is a real concern for women who are insecure.

This is why it is a smart idea for us to pinpoint the cause of our loneliness early on. Are we experiencing those undesirable feelings because honey pooh is not with us anymore? Or, are we feeling lonely because we desire something that we were not getting in the first place? Most times, if we dig deep enough, we will discover that loneliness is an emotional state that can be turned around, if replaced by true companionship that will last for eternity. Matthew 28:20 ideally demonstrates what true companionship looks like. It says it like this; *"I am with you always, even to the end of the age"* (NIV).

The Lord wants us to know, that He is right there by our side even through the relentless days and restless nights. He's able to provide whatever we're missing and then some. He's more than enough. Furthermore, when we allow the Lord to love on us, we won't get stuck in a relationship that could potentially delay our happiness and ultimately ruin the possibility of us ever having a successful future. As one popular television advertisement says, "You're in good hands with Allstate." I say, "You're in even better hands with the Lord."

Insecurity can be another impediment that plays a major role in determining which steps women will take to obtain a brighter future. Insecurity is also a factor in determining whether our actions will yield the results that we are hoping to get. "If we're afraid to jump, our parachutes will never open," according to famous author and talk show host, Steve Harvey. Harvey, also believes that, "All successful people had one thing in common; they jumped." If they had not jumped, the odds of being successful today would have been very slim.

When we lack confidence, people see us as worrywarts, timid, and even apprehensive. These are unfavorable qualities that are present when we are unsure of ourselves. We can be smart, good looking, and witty, yet insecure. It's the truth. We're afraid to do this and afraid to do that, so we don't give ourselves much room for human error. As a result, we tend to live our lives with "one toe in the water and the other on dry land." This can send mixed messages to our brain, the powerhouse of our bodies. If we don't know what we want or how to get it, it is difficult for us to come out of our shell. Sometimes, we're intimidated by the least little thing, and because of this, we often miss out on a chance of a lifetime to be used as a vessel of the Lord. If I were you, I would jump.

There are famous individuals that have admitted to having problems with insecurities in the past. We would have never guessed it if they hadn't said anything about it initially. This goes to show you that no one is exempt from this dilemma. Insecure people are afraid of taking chances. Thus, they allow the unknowns to govern a vast majority of their decisions. Individuals can also be insecure when they feel that they aren't equipped to handle certain situations effectively or live up to the expectations of significant others, which is all too common among women these days.

Finally, in additional to the barriers previously mentioned, women have also had to cope with educational and career setbacks. Sometimes the "woes" of life can be somewhat overwhelming. We know how hard our parents worked to put food on the table and clothes on our backs, yet we have somehow gotten ourselves into foolish situations that prevented us from obtaining an education or worse, advancing in our careers. Women have the smarts to receive a good education, and we certainly have the know-how to advance in the workplace. If the world had its way, I bet women would still be cooking and cleaning, meek and mild, and arrogant and average. If I had my way, women would continue to be spiritually sound, physically fit, and financially prepared for whatever comes our way.

Our problem is that we keep making costly mistakes. We don't show up for work on time, or not at all, we bicker back and forth with the boss lady, or we fail to meet specific deadlines. Why is this happening anyway? These careless behaviors are "deal breakers" in the workplace. The undertakings we experience often adds unnecessary stress to our already hectic lives. There are situations and circumstances that we have control over, but we wait until the last minute to rectify them. Whose fault is that?

My mother taught me to do "a bout face" when things are looking grim or appear hopeless. If you take my advice on this, either one or two things are sure to happen in your favor. You will shut the mouths of those doing the talking, or you will feel one-hundred percent better about yourself when things turn around. Ladies, please remember that we can't avoid the "woes" of life, but we can certainly advocate for ourselves in the meantime. Would you like to borrow my picket sign? I keep it in a safe place for times like this. You're more than welcome.

Exquisite Words of Wisdom

"A wise women wishes to be no one's enemy; a wise woman refuses to be anyone's victim." Maya Angelou

Here are five things you can do to avoid being a victim of your own circumstances:

1. *Once you realize you don't like the way things are going immediately try something different.*
2. *Try to recall how you got into that situation and vow not to ever do it again.*
3. *If you are hesitant about your resolution, go with your instinct.*
4. *Always do what's in your best interest.*
5. *Never look back.*

~QUESTION of the DAY~

How do you manage to get through the day when everything around you seems to be falling apart?

Affirmation: I am moving towards my destiny full speed ahead. I vow to keep on going no matter what others have said.
My afterthoughts concerning this affirmation are as follows:

_____

_____

_____

~Goal Setting Exercise~

My goal for not allowing the "woes" of life to get me down is to

_____

_____

My time-frame to accomplish this goal is

_____

_____

Once I have accomplished this goal, I plan to

_____

_____

~Reflections to Remember~

Oh, How Sweet it is: Recovering from Divorce and Defame

Letting go is one of the most difficult things we have to do even when we are unsure of where we're going to end up next.

Divorce can be extremely difficult for everyone including those who are not directly involved in the proceedings.

Forgiveness helps to heal the wounds of a broken heart. When we do not forgive, there is no way our hearts will ever completely heal.

~CHAPTER EIGHT~
Oh, How Sweet it is: Recovering from Divorce and Defame

How to avoid being bitter after divorce... forgive

Contrary to popular belief, nothing ever happens haphazardly in our lives. Everything we go through has purpose and meaning. Seldom do we enjoy the disappointment and pain, but in the end, there is much more for us to gain. When I finally came to grips with *that,* I found myself consistently reaching out to women who needed a shoulder to cry on, or a friendly smile to help make their day. Because I experienced that same kind of affliction, I would not have had it any other way. Most of them could not keep it together when their marriages had fallen apart. You could easily tell they had been through *hell* and needed a brand new start.

Many were stuck in a place of silence and yearned for someone who would care. After I finished telling my story, they knew that I would be there. We vowed not have a pity party or bash our ex-husbands for life. By the time we were done uplifting one another, we were determined not to have any strife. Our minds kept bringing us back to the times when our exes counted us out. We were on a mission to prove to ourselves that they didn't know what they were talking about. Some days, we would drop to our knees and pray to help us forget about the past. Then there were other days we refused to look back and girl we had a blast.

Take it from someone who has traveled down that same road before, it is not that easy to recover from a bitter divorce. So I promise not to set you up by pretending that everything was nice, but if you think divorce is easy, honey you better think twice. The wounds are sometimes so deeply engrained, that by the time you recover, your w-h-o-1-e outlook on life has changed. Your dreams and visions won't seem to matter as much, when you're all alone at night and you're missing his touch. His arms won't be locked around your teeny tiny waist, and his big luscious lips won't be kissing on your face.

We really don't know what will happen next, after everything falls apart. This is why we pray for strength and must have a forgiving heart. Prayer is what it takes to survive and we certainly need each other. Though we couldn't see eye to eye on most things, we had to respect one another. I know it's difficult for you to stay focused after all that you've been through, but concentrating on your release from bondage is something that you

MUST do. Kick off those shoes and put away that old purse—there is no need to remain in sorrow. Remember what I told you before, "THERE IS STILL HOPE FOR TOMORROW."

I am all for the idea of marriage between a man and a woman who have conscientiously and faithfully decided to be united as one. The lucky couple has my blessings indeed. I will even sing at the wedding if they wanted me to or start a line dance to entertain the entire crew. Who am I to discourage lovers from hooking up together? I just want you to be sure, my dear, that "Larry" is the right fellow.

Marriage was ordained by God. Never in a million years would I speak against anything that was established by Him. My only intentions are to share with you some of the experiences that I have gone through. I can show you how depending on the Lord can change your entire life. He can do miraculous things, but you must first overcome any strife.

As a woman, I care enough about you and the women that I just so happen to bump into, to allow you to get duked by those unpredictable pitfalls that often accompany a laborious divorce, like the one I experienced several years ago, but tried to hush-up by walking around with a phony smile on my face. You know how it is when we're flustered by life's calamities that hit us so hard that it makes us smile and cry at the same time. Yikes. What a scary sight. Can you imagine dark splashes of black eyeliner trickling down your nose and patches of midnight blue lipstick splattered all over your clothes? It reminds you of a scene from a horror movie or something.

Honestly, I don't know which is worst, going through a painstaking divorce or being told that you have an incurable disease. Both have the potential of zapping the life right out of you in a heartbeat. Then again, these disastrous misfortunes also have what it takes to encourage us to live every day like it's our last. So, let's forget about our not so perfect past, and run as fast as our legs will carry us towards a glorious future. Just think about what is out there waiting for you once you decide that you refuse to be held down by life's misfortunes?

Now that you are anxious and all excited about your promising future, let's pause for a second and take a deep breath before we get down to business. The reason I'm writing this chapter is *not* to share with you all of the grueling episodes that caused my marriage to end in divorce, but rather, to walk with you while you're going through, and to show you there is another choice. The choice that I'm referring to has nothing to do with being a "good" wife. Surely, what I'm about to share with you will remain with you for life. I am the one who can help you get through your misery and pain. So, pull yourself together girl and come in out of the rain. You do not need others to see those tears that keep rolling down your face. Grab a towel and dry your eyes, and get back in the race.

A marriage ending in divorce is one catastrophic crisis that you can never be fully prepared for. For starters, it is impossible to see all of the curveballs that are thrown at you while your emotions are having a pity party, not to mention that it can be a costly ordeal. You can't begin to imagine some of the controversial and emotionally charged feelings that flared up when I was in the middle of a lengthy divorce. Why did I have to endure so much hatred and pain? Can someone p-1-e-a-s-e tell me, what was there to gain? It turns out that my heartaches were preparing me to help women recover from their undeserving misery. My assignment is to mentor women who are recovering from suffering and shame. Now I can sit back and laugh at the Devil; I KNEW I WASN'T INSANE. Yet, I survived the loneliness, all the lies, and insecurity. Now every time that I look in the mirror; I JUST LOVE WHAT I SEE.

People from all "walks of life" would have you to believe that you will never be the same after going through a divorce. Regardless of who said it, I totally agree. My take on this is that once you experience a devastating divorce, how could you be the same? You can't. There is no way. It is my prayer that if you have chosen this route, you will be a brand new you once the dust settles. You will even think and act differently while doing things you never dreamed you could do, alone. The beauty of it all is that when you recover your life is bound to be on a different course. This time, you won't have to travel the course alone, so please don't think that all HOPE is gone.

Everyone goes through times of disappointment, but it depends on how well we handle those cloudy days and stormy nights. Our reactions to those mishaps will ultimately determine our fate. If we allow pain to destroy us, we lose. If we keep moving forward in spite of our pain, we win because we've conquered the very thing that was meant to defeat us. This was particularly true in my case.

When I first relocated back to my small hometown on the east coast, I can vividly recall my dad saying, "Everything that's good to you isn't necessarily good for you," during one of our many casual conversations that occurred almost daily. One thing I can certainly say about my dad; he was very good at giving advice. On top of that, he was an excellent cook. My dad made the world's best sweet potato pies. "Daddy Joe," as he was affectionately known by most of his friends, had grown to become a wise and whimsical character during his golden years. He was the *life* of the party, so to speak and could easily draw a crowd. "Daddy Joe" loved to be seen and heard, but he had good intentions. He merely wanted to add "a touch of spice" to the lives of those who frequently came in contact with him.

One thing about "Daddy Joe" he said what he meant and he meant what he said. He did not bite his tongue concerning anyone or anything. There were plenty of times when I witnessed him stand up to those who pretended to be cool, but after he'd finished telling them off, boy did they look like a fool. You never knew what would come out of his mouth, so we had to be very careful about what we told him, especially if we didn't want him to let the cat out of the bag. My mother would tell him all the time that, "he talked too much," but it didn't seem to bother him one bit. He just kept on laughing and grinning as he piddled around the house while waiting to chat with his next victim.

Anyone who spoke with my dad for any length of time wasn't about to escape his famous lectures. At times, I tried beating him to the punch by preparing myself for his unpredictable manner of speaking, hoping to keep our conversations short and sweet. No matter what, "Daddy Joe" was going to have the final word. The good thing about it was that my dad was right when giving advice most of the time. After all, he lived to be ninety-two years old and had a wealth of knowledge to share with anyone who would listen.

Most of dad's conversations were meant to keep the entire family on our toes and prepare us for the next great adventure. It never failed that when those old proverbs my dad used when proving a point were applied to our lives, somehow things would turn out just the way he said they would. "Daddy Joe" used to get a kick out being able to sit back and watch how his words of wisdom would always seem to come to fruition. Then, he would proudly say, "Didn't I tell you it would happen that way?"

Can you imagine how many headaches and low blows I could have actually avoided, if I would have kept that simple, but profound statement tucked away in the back of my mind; "Everything that's good to you isn't necessarily good for you?" Though it took a while, I knew exactly what my dad meant after my marriage failed and nearly caused me to lose hope. At the same time, we purposely ignore the sound advice of others and it comes right back around in full circles. As I look back over the heartaches and pain, I now realize I certainly should have listened more intently.

I'm almost certain that my dad's meaningful words could have prevented me from falling head over heels with the first man who promised me the world. As time went on, I later found out he was living in a world of his own, where everything revolved solely around him. "Where did I fit in?" I often wondered to myself. Why was I sitting around like a trophy on shelf? If I could turn back the hands of time, I would have given myself a chance to unwind. I would have taken time out to seek His face, instead of running down the aisle as though I was in a sack race.

Can you see why it is imperative that we consult with the Lord prior to getting twisted and tangled in something that we might later regret? This would certainly have prevented me from waking up in the middle of the night with my pillow all soak and wet. It's always good to talk to someone and sometimes to even wait. It would have definitely helped me to avoid a relationship that wasn't all that great.

While we're on the subject of life's struggles and bitter pills that women have to sometimes swallow, isn't it ironic that the things we were once gung ho over, somehow seems to slap us in the face when we least expect them too? All of us have said at one time or another, "THAT WON'T HAPPEN TO ME," but when it does, we're in a state of shock, even speechless. How many times have we said, "If only I had followed my mind the first time, this too could have been easily prevented?" My flesh was saying one thing, but my mind was telling me NO. The next time I will listen carefully to the ONE who told me so. "Yes," they were whispering. Some even tried warning me, but I was sick and tired of all the lies, SO I WANTED TO BE FREE. I knew one day, I would have my say to set the record straight. So, I kept my cool, didn't act a fool and now I'm doing GREAT. I was embarrassed to admit how hard I'd worked to keep my marriage together, but after years of contemplating how things went down; Dale just wasn't the right fellow.

If you have ever experienced anything close to this before, I know exactly how you must feel. No joke. It wasn't too long ago that I was standing in your shoes. My heart was crushed, just like yours. My dreams were even demolished just like yours, but once I saw the daylight, I could have kicked myself for being so senseless and stupid. What was the hurry? What was the rush? I could have avoided all the lies and definitely all the fuss. All I had to do was continue to wait and pray. I should have listened the first time and ran the other way. This is what happens when we get ahead of ourselves. Instead of taking it a step at a time, we start hearing wedding bells. When things don't turn out the way we planned, we ask ourselves a million times, "How did I fall in love with *that* man?" We must pull ourselves together if we're going to make it through. Aren't you tired of starting all over? Girl, I was too.

When we're unexpectedly hit from different directions with things that are out of our control, such as an indefensible marital affair or a messy divorce, it seems as though we can't put the pieces of our mangled lives back together. Most times when we try, we mistakenly make matters worse which is usually what happens when our marriages fall apart. It appears as though the pieces of our fragmented lives have been lost in the shuffle of a bad break-up, an unwarranted separation, or a spiteful divorce. The venomous pitfalls of a divorce are even more harrowing when there is no one around to help you settle down.

There are many heart-wrenching circumstances that we will experience at some point in our lives. Some can be avoided; some cannot. In Malachi 2:16, God declares that He hates divorce. Divorce is one of those debilitating experiences that can cause us a whole lot of frustration. To put it plainly, divorce is the death of a marriage. That is the only way I know how to explain it. Divorce and death are also synonymous in many ways. They both can leave a void in our lives that is very difficult to fill. I surmise this is why it takes a long time for us to be healed. Sometimes, even when we go on a shopping spree or to see a popular movie, our minds are still bombarded with the relationship that wasn't all that groovy.

Divorce and death are also compatible. Grieving the loss of a loved one occurs during both. Our hearts are split in two and we don't know what on earth to do. Then, there's the usual separation from a close-knit family unit as a result of a divorce.

Oh, How Sweet it is: Recovering from Divorce and Defame

Both men and women suffer tremendously from the remnants of a divorce so it's equally devastating. Their scars have the potential of lasting for years, even a lifetime, in some instances. Though divorce may affect men differently than women, it can leave us both feeling defeated, lonely, and cheated out of intimacy that was designed for a husband and wife. Divorce is so menacing that it causes envy and strife.

Divorce, has been known for contributing to chronic depression, mood swings, and even premature death when our hearts have been broken after a lengthy relationship has ended. I'm sure you've heard of someone dying from a broken heart, haven't you? Well, if you're in a relationship and things go sour, there is a strong possibility that your heart will also be crushed following a terrible break-up. There are news articles floating around all over the place explaining how someone has left this earth, as a result of a broken heart.

Additional side effects of divorce may include weight loss or weight gain, loss of appetite, and insomnia. Some of you may be thinking that weight loss or loss of appetite might not be so bad after all, but it can cause other areas of our bodies to suffer as well. Our immune system can also be affected by divorce. For example, when we are too exhausted to take care of our bodies properly, it begins to break down. Our limbs become weak. We walk around cranky when we're unable to sleep.

It has been said by many psychologists, that at least fifty percent of all marriages will end in divorce for one reason or another. Fifty percent is a very high number and seems to provide little or no hope for those who are contemplating marriage in the near future. Many people also believe that the divorce rate keeps getting higher every day, according to the information they've gathered from friends, colleagues, and of course the media. However, according to social researcher and author of *The Good News about Marriage*, Shaunti Feldhahn, "Fifty percent of marriages ending in divorce surfaced out of projections and that we have never gotten anywhere close to that misconception."[4] Feldhahn also believes that this data is a misrepresentation of the divorce rate. Therefore, people have been misled when it comes down to marriages falling apart.

No matter what percentage of marriages end in divorce, it is still too high. It's a shame we go out and spend what little money we do have on elaborate weddings, not to keep up with the Joneses, but to surpass them in an attempt to be remembered for having the wedding of the century. We end up regretting the day we walked down the aisle in front of three hundred witnesses. What's even worse is that we sometimes wind up regretting we ever met the guy we thought would be there for us during our golden years.

Actually, I could go on forever reiterating the numerous unsuccessful attempts to save my marriage, but that's not what matters now. What matters most, is that I continue doing everything within reason, to help women overcome the challenges that hinder their success. As you can see, divorce is unquestionably one of those challenges.

A divorce can be a major setback when everything comes at us all at once. Decisions, decisions, decisions! We must use wisdom.

Here's another word of caution; divorce is also one of the most catastrophic and painful ordeals that women will ever have to endure if there are small children in the home. Many times, there are innocent children involved in the whirlwinds of a devastating divorce. It's unfortunate that a child will also have to suffer from the heartbreak of this lethal weapon created by adults, but it happens more than you think. Sometimes there is no other way around it. If you and your spouse are contemplating divorce and there are small children in the picture, do yourselves and them an enormous favor; get some professional counseling lined up as soon as possible.

Professional counselors are a dime a dozen. They're the ones who are prepared for such daunting times. You can begin by first talking to the counselor at your child's school or church. By doing so, your child will benefit from the experience of hearing from another adult that "it isn't their fault this is happening to their family." Although a small child has bonded with his (or her) parents over the years, sooner or later he (or she) will need the intervention of another adult who can be trusted with his (or her) emotions during those dreadful times.

While divorce can be depleting at any age, it is my experience that women between the ages of thirty-five and forty-five usually have the worst time coming to grips with single parenthood. On the other hand, I have known women over the age of fifty who seem to have an easier time with divorce. More than likely, women in this age bracket are already financially secure and are in a better position to start a new career, a hobby, or to relocate, if need be. Equally as important, their children have probably gone off to college or have become young adults who have their own families to care for by now. Women within this category will probably stand a better chance of recovering from divorce and celebrating life as high-spirited and self-sufficient individuals, mainly because there is a good chance that they are accustomed to bouncing back from their struggles. Nevertheless, there is no easy way to get through the wear and tear of a pernicious divorce that is bound to knock the wind out of us with its inconceivable pain.

Moreover, when we're in our middle ages, women should enjoy spending quality time with our family and friends, while looking forward to advancing in various exciting career opportunities. We should also be preparing for a rewarding financial future later on down the road. Instead, many women will find themselves alone, financially drained, and sitting in divorce court if we're not serious about getting our lives together early on.

No one wants to be the loser in any situation, particularly in the case of a divorce, where two people have been married for many years. During the time they were together, their innermost secrets were exposed, leaving them vulnerable and at times insecure. Many hours were spent getting to know one another's likes, dislikes, and comfort levels in anticipation of securing a lifelong future together, until death due them part. Through the years, many couples have experienced the excitement and trials of raising successful children and even grandchildren together, while trying to maintain a happy and healthy marital relationship of their own.

It has been my understanding that a victorious person feels good on the inside about what he (or she) had accomplished. Most times, that individual will receive an award or a medal which they cherish for a lifetime in commemoration of their superior accomplishment. However, in the case of a divorce, no one walks away from the table with a trophy in his (or her) hand or a feather in his (or her) cap. More than that, it is difficult leaving a marriage without contemplating whether the right thing had been done. No matter who is at fault both parties stand to lose a lot. Unfortunately, it can take years recovering from the pain and destruction of a horrific divorce. It also takes more than a good cry to heal the tragedy of a broken heart that often lingers long after the final decree is signed.

Personally, I know of several individuals who are still recovering from a hideous divorce that occurred over four or five years ago. Not only have the ex-spouses lost their respect for one another, both individuals have lost family members and mutual friendships that were cultivated or developed over the course of their marriage. The loss of people, possessions, and things has ignited a fire of anger and rage, which can also take a lifetime to extinguish. How could their love for one another quickly turn to such hatred? All of those precious years as lovers, have been unintentionally wasted. They somehow grew apart and ended up with broken hearts. Unfortunately, this is how a dreadful divorce starts. Although divorce is a no-win situation, "OH, WHAT A RELIEF IT IS" to put those hostile feelings and dreaded memories behind, as we keep marching forward and vowing to do better the next time.

It is no secret that a divorce can have an overwhelming effect on the mind, body, and soul. The rollercoaster ride of emotional turmoil takes a toll on our ability to function at home, in the workplace, and most certainly in the community where we have to make decisions on the spot. If we are not snapping at our children and spouses, we're yelling and screaming at our co-worker who sits in the tiny cubical next to us. If not that, we're enraged at the local community watch meeting because things didn't go our way. We are not our usual selves when we're boiling over with anger, rage, and hatred. Though we try to put our past behind us, we must learn to forgive, if we want to receive *all* that our Heavenly Father has for us. Surely, it is impossible for us to enjoy a fruitful and balanced life when our actions are clearly pointing in the opposite direction.

I can remember being more than determined not to allow the side effects of a broken marriage ruin my life forever. I knew without a shadow of doubt that I had to get my life together. In order to avoid the backlash and negativity that was bound to come my way, I kneeled down slowly beside the bed and continued to quietly pray. It seems like yesterday that my marriage was under a hostile and brutal attack, but the more I thought about what I had to endure, there was no way that I was going back. The relationship crumbled like a stale oatmeal cookie right in front of me. When I signed the paperwork stating it was final, I was as scared as I could be.

At that time in my life, I was hurt, confused, and blazing hot with anger. It felt like steam was seeping out of my ears and nostrils simultaneously. As the steamy beads of water trickled down my bloated face, I looked towards the sky and yelled, "PLEASE HELP ME RUN THIS RACE." My mind was cluttered with unpleasant memories of a marriage that had gone sour. The way my life was going that day, I wouldn't have lasted another hour. I swore up and down I would do anything to turn my appalling life around, even if it meant that I wouldn't act real silly like "Bozo" the red nose clown. Life had given me lemons so I had to make lemonade. If I wanted to be an example for others, I certainly had to behave.

Divorce is also one of those dreaded disasters that can prevent anyone from enjoying the "simple" pleasures of life, which incidentally may differ from person to person. An individual may desire one thing to keep their mind occupied when going through a divorce, whereas, another individual may require something totally different, throughout the divorce process. The "simple" pleasures of life are golden opportunities in which we allow ourselves to enjoy something as simple as a soothing hot cup of ginger tea with honey and lemon or a freshly made peanut butter and jelly sandwich, with a tall, cold, glass of milk during an afternoon snack. I can smell the aroma of the piping hot tea that fills the room with its lemony fragrance. It reminds me that spring is in the air.

I can even imagine tasting some of those freshly hand-picked strawberries that make my favorite sandwich more worthwhile to eat. Can you tell me; when was the last time you enjoyed something so sweet? Go ahead. Think about it; but don't take too long. If it's taking you a while to answer, that's an indication it's been w-a-y too long. Don't you think that everyone should enjoy the "simple" pleasures of life, every once in a while?

By now, you are probably saying to yourself, "How did we come to talk about enjoying the simple pleasures of life in the middle of a chapter that should be teaching women about recovering from divorce?" What does one have to do with the other? Well, thank you for asking. This is another one of those meaningful life lessons that I want to share with you, to help keep your head above water. Surely, these words of wisdom will not go to waste. What better place and time, to discuss how women, can turn their lives around after having experienced a devastating divorce? Although divorce can prevent us from enjoying the simple things that once made our day, we have to somehow muster up the strength to keep on doing things the right way.

When something happens to us as traumatic as divorce, it also becomes next to impossible to appreciate anything that others do for us, although their intentions are good. Let's be honest. Sometimes we don't feel like being bothered with anyone or anything when we're going through something as mind-boggling as a divorce. We're not focused on the kind deeds that are done to uplift our spirits. We're too busy concentrating on the hurt we've unfairly experienced during a marriage that has been squashed. Furthermore, taking time out to entertain others during this remorseful period is the farthest thing away from our minds.

When we experience something as debilitating as divorce, our minds are set on either one or two things; quickly covering up the embarrassment and shame before anyone notices that we've been seriously wounded or strategizing how to bounce back from those childish episodes of name calling and finger pointing when it's all said and done. This is what makes us miss out on the "simple" pleasures of life.

During my lifetime, I have never heard of anyone who did not enjoy the simple things in life. These simplistic pleasures seem to fill our hearts with joy and laughter, after going through the drawbacks that keep us living on the edge. A hurtful divorce, the unexpected loss of a job, or the untimely death of a loved one, are all examples of difficult situations that makes us edgy. Furthermore, a heated argument, past due bills, or a wayward child can also cause us to almost lose it. Though women are often stunned by numerous demoralizing mishaps, I can certainly tell you that it has always been the "simple" pleasures of life that has kept a smile on my face.

Most women seem to enjoy the simple things in life. We love being pampered, but it's the simple things that have a lasting effect on us. Just to prove a point; can you even remember what gifts you received for Christmas last year? What about the ones that you got for your birthday, or on Valentine's Day? Now that you're scratching your head over this one, I bet you *can* remember the deliciously tasting homemade pound cake that the little old lady down the street made for you when she heard you weren't feeling well, can't you? Or what about that old beige and brown ceramic dish with the words "I Love You" carved in the center, that was given to you by the little boy in your Sunday School class? I bet you remember them both. My point exactly. It was those "simple" little pleasures that meant the most and certainly helped to make your day go much smoother. Shouldn't you take time to enjoy some of the "simple" pleasures that are around you every day?

I have noticed that when our thoughts have been shifted from pleasure to pain, we tend to forget all about the little things that we relish most. Although we all have a chance to enjoy the little things that may seem so insignificant to others, many women forfeit this opportunity when they have been deeply wounded and scared. Our scars are so deeply rooted that it is nearly impossible to cover them up. Whether we know it or not, most people can see right through the covers anyway, so why do we keep trying to hide them?

A few years ago, the mere thought of the word "divorce" would have caused me to stop in my tracks and do a little soul searching of my own. What would I have done if I'd suddenly become single? Thank God, I was adamant about taking time to wade through the cobwebs of confusion and chaos, prior to making any radical decisions that I might later regret. A hellish divorce is something you will never forget. It is a very scary feeling to go through such a boisterous experience without first praying and seeking guidance from the Lord. Divorce isn't something that any of us should applaud. If I had not sought the Lord every step of the way, I would not have been healthy and happy today. Though He hates divorce, this I know. He still loves me from head to toe.

There were many times when I felt lonely, broken, and rejected. I didn't think I would ever smile again. At times, I walked around like a zombie without a care in the world. I can also recall the resentment that I had towards those who seem to have their families in tack. I LITERALLY HATED THE SIGHT OF THEM. I could not stand to see them shopping together at the local grocery store, nor husbands and wives sharing a moment of intimacy while smooching and holding hands. I was insanely jealous and felt that I had been wrongfully cheated out of one of life's most simple pleasures.

As women, we can easily get wrapped up and entangled in many controversial situations that we wish would somehow just go away. What really matters most is what we do to make the best of those nerve-racking circumstances, even in the case of a deplorable divorce. When we don't take time to sift through the rubbish, our problems grow deeper and even more cumbersome. This is why most of us repeatedly run into the same problems. We fail to take time to discover who we really are and what we truly want. Moreover, we have allowed people and situations such as divorce, loneliness, and low self-esteem to dictate our futures. When are we ever going to break this vicious cycle that seems to curl up in our beds right next to us at night?

Shortly after my divorce, I decided that my singleness did not define who I was, nor did it dictate my future success. Frankly, as oddly as it may seem, this tragic situation made me stronger and wiser. It enabled me to stand in my truth and face my fears. I didn't have to pretend to be something that I wasn't, nor did I have to pretend to have something that I did not have. I finally had the opportunity to experience the real me, and I LOVE IT! There was nothing to be ashamed of anymore and no one could hold anything over my head. On top of that, the divorce strengthened my relationship with the Lord. It also helped me to see that the Lord was true to His word when He said, "He would always be there for me." Under those circumstances, there was no way that a tormenting divorce would ever hinder me from helping other women to overcome their fears and insecurities. After all, I WAS BORN TO DO THIS. My cry for help became a cry for HOPE. I finally conquered the fear of loneliness, depression, and low self-esteem. Now, I am proud to hold my head up high, instead of walking around looking grumpy, unpleasant, and mean.

In the midst of the turmoil that lasted for months it was extremely challenging to remain level-headed and calm, although I managed to somehow survive when everyone else had counted me out. The word was out all over town that I wouldn't make it through *this* one. For a moment, I was beginning to wonder if there was any truth to what was being said. After all, I had been misled. This time, I was going to have a conceivable plan in place. There was no way I was going to walk away with mud all over my face. Sometimes I would stay up all night long while contemplating my next move. Since my desire was to have some peace in my life, my plan had to be brilliant and smooth.

Moreover, if you are going to survive the tough times after divorce, you will also need some money in the bank, which I will discuss at length in the coming chapters. I'm not saying that you will need a million bucks on hand, although that would be rather nice. What I am telling you is that you will definitely need to have an emergency fund where your money is *always* accessible to you. You never know when your ex is going to act like a fool. If you do not have any funds in the bank, or in an old torn up shoebox underneath the bed, you're just asking for trouble. You may not have nearly as much as you desire, but it will be there when you need it most. That's what important. Divorce is one of those unfortunate situations where you could probably stand to have two or three emergency funds at your disposal, if you ask me. This is one expense you do not want to incur; especially if you're running on empty.

Whatever you do, you must also guard your heart, so that your life won't be torn apart, by people who often make promises they don't intend to keep. You must grow up now young lady, and never miss a beat. Aren't you tired of starting your life all over and over again; after loving someone who you thought was cool and pretended to be your best friend? Hold your head up high, even if you have to cry. The Lord will wipe those tears away in preparation for the right guy.

I dreaded having to start my complicated life all over again. I knew it was going to be vicious and tough so I had no choice but to win. I started out wondering to myself, "How could this happen to me?" Then, I finally settled down one day and decided to wait to see. After wading through all of the confusion, it wasn't so bad after all. A few years before, I was scared to death, but now I am having a ball.

In addition to the critical matters that I just spoke of, you are definitely going to need the guidance of the Lord, as I have referenced throughout the entire book. There is no fancy way to put it. You will surely need Him to comfort you through the agony and pain of a traumatizing divorce. You have read about all of the marvelous things that He has done for me. He filled my soul with joy and laughter so that it would not be empty.

Now everywhere I go, people want to know, is this really me. I smile at them and softly say, "I'm not the same as I used to be." They ask me, "What could they do right now to get their lives back on track?" I gently whisper in their ear, "There's no turning back."

In concluding this chapter, I would like to leave you with some final words to help strengthen your faith. Before I do, I want to reiterate that I am in no way advocating divorce. That's not even the point of this chapter. I am merely providing you words of comfort to ensure that you remain strong and steadfast through any crippling situation. Divorce is just one of those distressing situations that you might have to endure. Face it; life happens. When it happens to us, we must focus on the solution, not the problem. However, the right solution to any problem can be more agonizing than we can ever imagine, if it doesn't involve the Lord.

Recovering from defame as a result of a cruddy divorce is by far one of the most draining experiences that any of us might have to encounter, regardless of our financial status, accomplishments, or positions that we hold within the community. The entire divorce process can be grueling and grossly mishandled, leaving our minds messed up, hearts crushed, and purses (or wallets) empty. Most times, we are in a HOPELESS state of mind when we're faced with the aftermath of the scars it leaves.

The emotional piercing of one's heart can be perceived as worse than death. Moreover, the residue from this laborious undertaking has been known to linger on forever. As in any case, there are exceptions to every rule. My prayer is that you are the exception. Therefore, if by chance you do find that your marriage is about to end in divorce, do not cry, S.M.I.L.E. (Start Meditating on Irrefutable Life Experiences) instead. Focus your attention on the new life ahead of you. *"Trust in the Lord with all thine heart. Lean not unto thine own understanding. In all thine ways acknowledge him and he shall direct your path"* (Proverbs 3:5 NIV).

~Question of the Day~

Things do not always go as planned. Most times, if we are not careful they can catch us off guard. How do you handle life's unexpected occurrences?

_____

_____

_____

Affirmation: I will stand on the solid rock that keeps me from sinking even though my troubles are threatening to toss me overboard.
My afterthoughts concerning this affirmation are as follows:

_____

_____

~Goal Setting Exercise~

My goal for turning my life around after experiencing hurt is to

_____

_____

_____

My time-frame to accomplish this goal is

_____

_____

_____

Once I accomplish this goal, I plan to

_____

_____

_____

_____

~Reflections to Remember~

Look no Further: He's the One

The one who feeds our mind also feeds our soul.

When you are looking for something that will sustain you for life be sure to search the panels of your heart. That is the place where truth resides.

Loving without limits simply means taking your foot off the brakes when trouble comes.

~CHAPTER NINE~

Look no Further: He's the One

How not to settle for the wrong guy

Relationships are supposed to last, but when they don't, where does that leave us? Some of us are left without a date, with no shoulder to cry on, and no one to buy us fancy chocolates on Valentine's Day. Here's what makes it even worse: if we're afraid of being alone, we might end up with the wrong guy living in our home. Instead of waiting on Mr. Right, we end up settling for Mr. Right Now. Incidentally, he's the same guy we've been dating all along. The only difference is his last name and he enjoys talking on the telephone.

How many of you are brave enough to admit that you're still waiting on your Boaz? Go ahead; raise them higher. For those who raised your hand, thank you for your honesty. I'm quite certain there are others out there who are afraid of divulging the truth. You don't have to be ashamed to let the world know that you want somebody to love. Spending time with someone you adore is a natural part of life.

Sometimes though, waiting can turn into long periods of wondering if Boaz really exists. Well ladies, in order to ease the doubt that might be running through your mind at times; Boaz *does* exist. The question is; where *is* he? More importantly, what's taking him *so* long?

In the book of Ruth, Boaz is described as a wealthy landowner who believed in the Lord. He's also depicted as a protector, provider, and a man of integrity. When reading the touching love story of Boaz and Ruth it can easily be surmised that he was strong, caring, and compassionate to boot. If you ask me, Boaz sounds just like the mighty man of valor that all of us have been longing for. However, some of us have given up on the idea of spending the rest of our lives with the man of our dreams because Boaz hasn't shown up yet. But, what if he doesn't? Can you make without him?

Incidentally, you don't have to go out on the town searching for a "man." Believe me; he will find you. Most times, he'll show up on your door step even when you don't want him to. It behooves us to be careful about those whom we chose to spend the rest of our lives with. It's quite easy these days to be misled by someone who brings us gifts. "Everything that glitters certainly isn't gold; men will come and men will go."

My dear sister, you must be wise in everything you say or do or it might come back to haunt you. If you're searching for the "man" of your dreams look no further. Proverbs 18:22 tells us that; *"He who finds a wife, finds a good thing, and obtains favor from the Lord"* (NKJV). It's not the other way around. Some of us have definitely got it twisted. We fall in love on the very first date, but when he doesn't ask us to marry him, we immediately become irate. Don't you know that a woman like you is fearfully and wonderfully made? This is *not* the way that a lovely lady is supposed to behave.

I realize that women are emotional and super sensitive. Because of this, we are sometimes head over heels about the men of our dreams. Could it be that we're afraid of being alone so we hop from one relationship to another without first thinking about where it might take us in the future? Moreover, some of us don't even believe that we have a future without Boaz. It's not that Boaz isn't a great guy. We all know that he is. What gets us into trouble is settling for the wrong guy, when Boaz is taking his sweet little time coming our way. We're unable to think logically when our minds are all over the place. Most times, we say and do things that often slap us in the face. We're here, there, and everywhere. Sometimes we're up, down, and always wearing a frown. This is how we allow others to take advantage of us when we're acting like a clown. Obviously, we don't have our thinking caps on straight when we need them most. Remember what I told you earlier, "Stop acting like a ghost."

We cannot allow our emotions to prevent us from thinking clearly or we will pay for it dearly. There have been many times that I had to keep my emotions in check and my mouth shut to avoid getting into a rut. There have also been times that I had to think my way through painful situations that otherwise could have driven me crazy. One tiny mistake and my life could have been over just like that.

While we are on the touchy subject of finding our soul mates, I have to admit that women give our all to those whom we deeply care about. That's a given. It just comes naturally for most of us. We go out of our way to make sure everything is just right so we overlook inappropriate behavior and disrespect as though they were out of sight. Although we want things to work out for the best, sometimes we intentionally ignore the red flags that cause us a BIG mess.

I wonder why women are vulnerable to things we have the power to overcome. Are we that desperate to be in a relationship with a man that it causes us to doubt our capabilities as a woman? Why do we continue lowering our standards to appease some guy who doesn't deserve the time of day anyway? Of course, I'm not referring to Boaz. He's the exception. Ladies, our lives are more precious to us than that, even if we're the only ones who feel this way. You and I can't be so trusting that we give the green light to every Tom, Dick, or Harry. We certainly don't want him destroying what has already been built up inside of us. "No way Hosea" as my dad used to say when he was not about to bulge because his mind had already been set in stone.

Did you know that each time we allow someone in and out of our lives they take a little piece of us with them whether it's good or bad? Some tend to chip away at our innermost being when the relationship goes sour. When we're crushed and walked all over or even left hanging out to dry, sooner or later, the little bit of self-confidence we did have will almost become nonexistent. We must safeguard the treasure of *life* that the Lord has freely given us as well as protect our emotions. Although this sounds like a difficult task, we have no other choice if we want to enjoy our lives to the fullest.

Life is a precious commodity that we must not take for granted. We do not need the wrong guy to zap the *life* out of us in a split second. We're supposed to spread *joy* and give *hope* to other women who have literally given up. We owe it to one another as women. Why do we keep handing over our lives to some joker who's barely making it himself? It took a long time for me to figure that one out, almost two decades to be exact. Then, I finally got it. I finally realized that the Lord had already affirmed me. Therefore, if I needed any more reassurance than that, all I had to do was to look to THE MAN, JESUS CHRIST, not a "man" as the world would have it.

If women would get rid of that old crusty mentality that "having a man to depend on is a great financial plan" or that false image concerning "a house is not a home if you live there alone" we'll be better off. HONESTLY. Let's think about this for a moment and discuss these silly misconceptions one by one. Does having a "man" in your life means that you will have a solid financial plan in place for the future? IF YOU THINK IT CAN; YOU BETTER THINK AGAIN. We're equipped to build our own financial futures and to leave an inheritance for our children's children, without the help of a "man" who snores in our faces at night. Isn't this one of the reasons we work so hard in the first place, so we can at least get some of the things we desire?

Contrary to popular belief, research says that one of the main reasons relationships fail is not attributed to the absence of money in the household, but rather, not having *enough* money to sustain the relationship itself. Common sense should tell us when couples start out pinching pennies, this is a sure sign their relationship is heading for trouble. It is also an indication that some fine-tuning needs to be done to steer the couple in the direction of financial freedom. A heart-to-heart conversation about their finances should have taken place long before the marriage proposal was accepted. Unfortunately, some couples fail to have this "much needed" dialogue until after they have said, "I do." Then, they start to quickly wonder, "Who in the world am I married to?"

Heated discussions surrounding a couple's finances can often lead to finger pointing and jumping down one's throat when they don't see eye to eye on how their money should be spent. He says she's spending every time she gets paid; she says he's spending just to make the ladies wave. Both of them are finding fault with one another when on the other hand they should be helping each other. Poor money habits can tear any relationship apart. Therefore, it behooves a man and wife to have their finances together from the start.

If we have any doubts about whether or not we have what it takes to get our finances in order or what investments we'll need to make, the next best thing for us to do is seek professional assistance. I did it. I hired an awesome financial advisor to help me along the way. I also became an avid reader of financial planning guides and carefully researched sound advice given by a variety of influential people who hosted their own television shows focusing on financial wellness. It has certainly expanded my financial awareness. Since I took it upon myself to become knowledgeable in this arena, I'm prepared for whatever comes my way, financially speaking that is.

I'm not saying that you have to instantly become a financial expert. However, I will say that you must take time for getting your finances in order. There are plenty of free and reputable agencies out there that will be more than happy to help you get started. You can't beat that. Here is one of my favorite mottos that I live by and have committed to memory. It will help you in getting your priorities straight. Post this powerful quote on your vision board or tape it to your mirror, so that you'll be reminded how to keep your finances in order; "Proper prior planning prevents poor performance." I refer to it as the six P's. If you think about the underlying message that it holds prior to making decisions about your finances, you won't have any regrets.

Furthermore, if we think we have the perfect "man" in our lives, there is *no* way he can substitute for our financial well-being in the near future. He probably doesn't make that kind of money, or if he does, you better believe he already has plans for it that most likely doesn't include us. Let's stay on the safe side and stick with what we know works.

For one thing, we know for sure that obedience to the Word of God, works on the behalf of our families, futures, and our finances. Romans 8:28 puts it this way; *"And we know that all things work together for good to them that love God, to them who are called according to his purpose"* (KJV). I'm sure by now you have experienced numerous miracles in your life that the Lord has done for you personally, professionally, and financially; probably too many to count if you really want to know the truth. That means you're on the right track. Let's continue trusting the Lord with our finances, as well as everything else. He's the type of "man" we all need by our side.

Consequently, when we falsely believe that having a "man" in our lives is a sure way of guaranteeing a comfortable financial future, that's like comparing apples to oranges. What does one have to do with the other? There are dozens of women out there who would tell you this way of thinking is bizarre and downright crazy. Many women still struggle financially although they have a "man" in their lives so we know this is not the case. On the contrary, there are women, who truly believe the man they love is all they need. Unfortunately, they are focusing on the materialistic things that he is capable of providing for them right now. Regardless of whether some women chose to believe this nonsense, we have been taught better. When we know better, we do better, right?

Now, let's discuss that old adage most women including me have feared for years; "A house is not a home if you live there alone." Truthfully, I don't even know where that originated, do you? Nevertheless, it has been around for a while. I heard others refer to it on more than one occasion. I knew exactly what they meant when the said it. However, I want to take it a step further. Hopefully, our little chat will ease your anxieties when it comes to being alone.

Tell me, how *does* living in a house alone *not* make it a home? Does that make any sense at all? Let's talk this through together. My desire is to help you and other women overcome your fears regarding this commonly talked about misconception as well. You never know, you or I just might end up living our lives alone from now on. What I mean by this is that there is a strong possibility at some point in our adult lives we might reside in a home without the presence of a male companion. If you think about it, that might not be so bad after all. There is one thing for sure, we have the same opportunity of turning our houses into homes, just like everyone else, whether we have a "man" living there with us or not. If the truth be told; some married women wish they were living alone at times, and are not ashamed to admit it. Uh-oh, why is *that* look on your face? Did I say something wrong?

We can easily see how a house and a home are synonymous and used as a primary place of residence for its occupants. If there's only one individual living in *that* particular structure, would that change its primary purpose? Think about it. Moreover, if there were two or more individuals occupying *that* same structure, would that even change the reason for which *that* structure was built? The answer is *no* to both questions. Then, how could that old saying possibly be true?

Furthermore, a house can be referred to as "a single family structure which is situated on a solid foundation, whereas its contents, environment, and personality provides a more personal feeling for its occupants," regardless of the number. The occupants are also able to develop a sense of belonging in a welcoming environment within their place of residence. Individuals residing in the home are free to make changes that will suit their particular personalities, moods, and interests whenever they desire. This is what makes it a home, not the amount of people residing in it, and certainly not the fact that a "man" doesn't live there with us, as it is frequently implied. Now you have it? This is one less thing that you and I will ever have to worry about since we know the truth.

Here's another piece of advice for you while I have your undivided attention. You better think twice before taking that eternal vow that some women are anxiously awaiting to take. If you run down that aisle too quickly, you could be making another grave mistake. Some women have taken years to meticulously plan what others have

Look no Further: He's the One

referred to as "the wedding of the century" only to find themselves in divorce court in less than seventy-two hours. It turns out that their outrageously overpriced marital ceremony was only a show, so that the whole world would know.

Some of us find it hard to be content without a "man" in our lives. We'll do just about anything under the sun to keep him happy—even telling lies. What is it about women that make us jump to his every command? Are we *that* headstrong and determined to be with any old man? This may sound harsh, but it is true. Without a man in our lives, some of us wouldn't know what to do.

When it comes to women and relationships, we look for love in all the wrong places. If things don't turn out right, we go around with disgruntled faces. What is it going to take for us to finally realize, that the very thing we're looking for, is right in front of our eyes? How long will we continue to search for that wealthy and perfect man? Do we really need some old guy to hold us by the hand?

Ladies, isn't it about time that we give it rest? Why do we keep on looking for a man to help us feel our best? I realize that you are picky and you want things to go your way so I've got just the right *man* for you who will brighten up your day. He's meek and mild and such a cool gentleman. He never operates haphazardly; He always has a plan. He'll listen when you speak and even rock you fast to sleep. He knows exactly what to do and He's waiting just for you. Look no further; He's the one. His name is JESUS CHRIST, THE ONLY BEGOTTEN SON.

So, what will you do now that He's looking for you? Will you turn your back on Him when you're feeling sad and blue? Not only will He help you to get rid of any strife; He'll pick you up and turn you around, and give you eternal life. Tell me what woman in her right mind would not want a man like Him, who's quite capable and willing to take good care of them? You don't need to dress up pretty or put on a wild show. Everything about you, trust me, He already knows.

Stop looking for a "man" who can break your heart in two. You can spend the rest of your life with JESUS, without even saying, "I do." He is right there when you need Him, especially when it's dark. He's even by your side when you're walking in the park. He's a friend of the friendless and hope for us all. Girl if you have a "man" like JESUS, you'll have yourself a ball.

Jesus has his hands out waiting for someone like you. Stop scratching your head and looking around; you know what you have to. Just hold on tight; He'll treat you right. He loves you unconditionally and He thinks you're out of sight. Look no further; He's the one. His name is JESUS CHRIST, THE ONE AND ONLY SON.

Exquisite Words of Wisdom

"Being single doesn't mean no one wants you; it means God is busy writing your love story." Julia Hoxie

Here are seven things you can do while you are waiting on your Boaz:

1. Get to know God.
2. Get to know yourself.
3. Learn a foreign language.
4. Travel the world.
5. Start your dream business.
6. Make someone else's dream come true.
7. Pray for wisdom.

~Question of the Day~

Most times, when we are searching for the right thing that will satisfy our needs, the very thing that will do the trick is usually right there in front of us. How do you feel when you have found just what you needed to make it through the day?

_____

_____

Affirmation: While in search of my destiny, I will focus on building an eternal relationship with the "man" who holds the key to my future. He's Jesus Christ, Our Lord and Savior.
My afterthoughts concerning this affirmation are as follows:

_____

_____

~Goal Setting Exercise~

My goal for maintaining a special relationship with the Lord is to

_____

_____

My time-frame to accomplish this goal is

_____

_____

Once I accomplish this goal, I plan to

_____

_____

~Reflections to Remember~

Faithful, Frugal, and Fabulous

Developing a spending plan is easy. Maintaining allegiance to it is the difficult part.

Overspending to gain someone's attention rarely works. However, underspending is bound to get them talking.

Saving for the future is never easy. Neither is having a future without any savings.

~CHAPTER TEN~
Faithful, Frugal, and Fabulous

*How not to be broke, busted, and disgusted
before and after retirement*

Living in poverty is a major fear many women might have to face at some point in life. The effects of poverty are often interconnected so that there is no single problem that exists because of it. Sadly a multitude of problems erupt when our money runs out. As a result, bad situations evolve and eventually turn into lifelong disasters that could have been avoided, if proper money management skills were in place. Grant it, no one enjoys living from paycheck to paycheck, but regrettably this scenario is all too common when we constantly mishandle our money.

From time to time, a serious conversation about our finances needs to take place although it is usually out of the question when we're barely making ends meet as it is. However, this dreaded discussion *must* occur whether we like it or not.

We cannot run from our financial situation no matter how bleak the future looks when our funds aren't where they should be. This is what's been happening to some of us for years. Due to carelessness and a lack of knowledge, poverty has taken its toll.

Now that you are on the verge of recovering from the death trap of hopelessness that almost cost you your life, isn't it time you started thinking about your future? This conversation is not about a romantic cheek-to-cheek relationship with your significant other. That is not where I am headed here. There is plenty of time for that. Save the thought of you and him spending the rest of your lives together until you can at least see yourself halfway through the financial bind you may be in right now. Your head must be on straight first before you can even begin thinking about having a companion in your life. If you really want to destroy a relationship, start having money problems early on and you'll see just how fast the courtship will end.

What would your relationship look like if neither you nor your significant other has money left over for spending after being paid? You know that's what happens to a large percentage of people. Since we don't use proper money management skills our money slips through our fingers as fast as we can make it. Well, let me tell you something, honey; money and men don't mix, when you don't have any of your own. So, let's put the brakes on spending or your spending habits will definitely break you.

If I sound upset, you're absolutely right. I have seen women on numerous occasions blow money on "stuff" they already have around the house or tucked away somewhere in the basement. It is obvious it wasn't purchased out of necessity since it hasn't been touched in years. Here's something for you to think about; people are living well past the age of eighty these days which means they're out living their nest egg that they saved up for retirement. This is definitely a huge concern. By the way, are you financially prepared to take care of your needs when no one can or will? If you can't you'll need a little reality check to ensure your financial obligations are definitely going to be met. Trust me, you will be the one that has to make it happen.

Have you begun thinking about retirement, or how you will survive once you no longer have a nine to five? You better put some funds away for tomorrow will surely come. You don't want to end up out on the street being labeled as a bum. Proper money management has its advantages when we are in control of our finances, especially if we're nearing the ripe old age of sixty-five. Boy, does that seem like a long ways off for some of us. Unfortunately, for many, it's just around the corner.

Some of us might as well get prepared to work a little longer, maybe even past the age of seventy, due to poor budgeting habits when it comes to planning for the future. One of the main reasons can be attributed to immediate gratification during our younger years when we thought it was cool to go out shopping for clothes or shoes every weekend. We didn't have a clue about the value of money back then and some of us still don't. When we finally realized how little we did know about saving; our purses were already running on empty and our bank accounts closed. Who wants to end up in a situation where we're forced to continue working when we really want to quit?

In order to understand how imperative it is that we are good stewards over our money, Proverbs 6:6–11 offers us wisdom concerning what happens if we ruin our finances. This very informative book of the *Bible* also warns us about the potential of becoming a "sluggard" who prefers not to work at all. If a person squanders his (or her) money this irresponsible behavior will lead to financial ruin no matter how you look at it. Have your finances also by chance taken a serious hit? If your money situation is not where it should be as over fifty percent of women today, it's never too late to get your financial house in order. Let's grab another cup of coffee while we discuss the importance of being financially stable both before and during retirement.

Can you tell me when was the last time you took a g-o-o-d look at your bank account? Is it in good standing? Or, have you overdrawn it three times just this year alone? Overdrafts can be expensive if you are not good at handling money, you know. If you're fortunate enough to have an account at one of the million banks we have around here, that's a good thing. My concern is that you know how to read your monthly statements and learn how to properly manage your money. If you don't know how to read the monthly statement, how are you keeping track of the funds you're supposed to have saved up for the unexpected? Why the puzzled look, my friend? This nonchalant attitude concerning your money must now come to an end. I only want to share with you how *you* can get it all together. Your finances should be important to *you* no matter what the weather. Everyone has their ups and downs; that's just the way life goes. This is why I am talking to you, so that you can stay on your toes.

Getting our financial houses in order can be a daunting task if we do not know where to begin. Sadly, some of us don't even care to begin. Some women would prefer cooking or cleaning or watching our favorite nighttime soap operas rather than having anything to do with our finances. Some of us even cringe when the bills are due, but surely, you do not want this to be you.

Moreover, haven't you heard of individuals who were favored with a large windfall and soon afterwards, they were flat broke? Either one or two things happened; they were spending uncontrollably or they ended up giving their money away to long lost relatives that popped up out of the blue. Sounds bizarre, doesn't it? Well, it's the truth. I do not want this to be your story, too.

It's no secret that some women have had a difficult time dealing with finances. For starters, we've handed over the financial responsibility to our husbands or significant others. In some cases, we're too busy caring for what seems to matter most, our families. Could it be that we simply don't have the financial know-how, so it's just easier for someone else to take charge and lead the way? Why can't we become good stewards of our own money and pay what needs to be paid? It is my prayer that the information, financial tips, and strategies I'll share with you in this chapter will change all of *that,* so you can begin handling your own money instead of depending on the man who wears the hat.

There is one thing I want to say to you up front. We cannot be afraid of handling our money no matter how much or how little of it we may have. It's going to take someone you can trust to tell you the truth about the way you manage your finances so that you won't end up in poverty. At this stage of the game, I have taken the liberty to do so. Yes, me. You can take notes from someone who has experienced carelessness with money, but has now gotten her financial affairs in order. I'm proud to admit that I am on top of things when it comes to my net worth. It wasn't an easy chore, but now I can celebrate. Don't you want to join me?

Do you remember when I told you that I struggled to get to where I am right now? Well, I wasn't kidding you. Managing my finances properly took several years of planning, discipline, and research, but it paid off. Yes, it took a while, but I had guts enough to shift gears before corruption set in. You think not having any money is bad; try asking someone for a ride to work for a couple of days when you don't have the funds to get your own vehicle fixed. You'll see what I mean. To help me get a grip on making sure that I was in a good place financially, I read every single financial guide I could get my hands on, attended multiple seminars, and even had a heart-to-heart talk with myself. I wanted different results so I began handling my finances differently. Essentially, I began to *think* differentially. In essence, this was the key to turning my finances around.

Although money is a valuable must-have for survival, it is nothing to play with. You must do as I did and face the truth regarding your finances no matter how dismal the circumstances may appear. For some, it might not be so pretty, but at least you'll know where you stand before detriment comes peering through your window. It catches up with all of us who fail to initiate a financial plan. Prior to us going into details about how this tedious, yet necessary, task is done let me put a little bug in your ear. We do not have the ability, or the foresight to produce wealth, as most of us have been led to believe. It takes someone *extra* special to do that for us.

Deuteronomy 8:18 says it like this; *"But remember the Lord your God, for it is he who gives you the ability to produce wealth, and so confirms his covenant, which he swore to your ancestors, as it is today"* (NIV). Therefore, if you want to build wealth and get your finances together simultaneously, just ask the Lord.

If there was ever any confusion concerning where our finances come from; I hope by now you've figured it out. Many believe it is their jobs or bank accounts, that provide for them. However, *we* know better. The truth is both of these high-ranking necessities have failed us immensely in the past. It is the Lord who gives us the power to obtain wealth *and* the knowledge we need for handling our money properly. Our responsibility is to please Him in every way; which also includes being a good steward over the funds He has so graciously entrusted to us.

Though having a solid financial plan should be important to everyone, it is imperative that women of all ages do not miss the boat when it comes to properly managing our money. We don't have time to play around with this aspect of our lives. It is crucial that we learn how to take care of our own financial needs for the future. If we cannot trust ourselves with our money, then who can we trust? Certainly, not a stranger who cannot make heads or tails out of his (or her) own finances. Proverbs 16:3 establishes this clearly when it tells us to *"Commit to the Lord whatever you do, and he will establish your plans"* (NIV). This means *everything* including our money.

When I was growing up, I can recall my parents working together so that the bills were paid on time and we had a little money in the bank, just in case. I never knew how much nor was I about to ask. Poking our noses in the business of adults was not the thing to do around my house. All I know is that my mom would have a *fit* if the money wasn't in the bank when she needed it to be. This was how I learned the importance of saving at a very early age. I was taught not to spend every nickel and dime that came my way.

In my childhood days, I didn't even think about emergencies, did you? I was either outside playing with my friends or stuck in a corner somewhere reading a book. I left that up to my parents to worry about, not me. Although it was tempting to spend without thinking, I had sense enough to put some money away. My mom would tell us that our money had to stretch. At first, I did not quite understand, but as I grew older, I found out exactly what was meant by that. Now, I am able to help women get their finances together before *all* of their money is spent.

One of the reasons I decided to focus on finances was because I've repeatedly seen women fighting a losing battle when it came down to their money. I was also tired of getting beaten up by my own financial situation. I needed something to change in a hurry. We are in a tizzy when we realize the money we *thought* we had has somehow gotten away from us. Sadly, we couldn't even tell you where it went if our lives depended on it. It is also a scary place to be, so please listen carefully to me. By the time we finally decide to turn our financial situations around it's almost too late. It strikes us like a bolt of lightning that doesn't feel so great. I would not be telling you this if I hadn't experienced it for myself. Now that I got my finances in order, I am steadily building wealth.

There was a time in my life when I wasn't as savvy about my finances as I am today. I'm not ashamed to tell the world that my mind was on everything else except my financial well-being. Somehow, for years I was able to pretend that

I had it all together, financially speaking that is, but who was I fooling? I continued living as though everything was okay, just as some of you are doing as we speak. You know how it is when things have gotten out of control, but we're too afraid to ask for help because of the repercussions and ridicule that comes along with it. This is one of the main reasons we ignore the bad news about our finances as if it does not exist. We put our blinders on because we're afraid of what we might otherwise see. We put our earplugs in because we're afraid of what we might hear. At least that's what I did for a while. Then, it hit me. I had better do something fast in order to prevent a financial disaster from coming my way. Since the future of my retirement was at stake, I did not have any more time to waste.

When I first became aware of the problems with my finances, I was mainly focused on the tutorial business that ended up being a very arduous task. The business had recently opened at the time, so I could not afford to hire an assistant. There was no other choice, but to be creative and resourceful with the funds I had at my disposal. Thankfully, I opted not to take out a business loan from the local bank. Instead, I was fortunate enough to use the funds from my personal account to maintain, until the proceeds started rolling in. Furthermore, I did not want the responsibility of having to pay it back.

A situation as such would have definitely harmed my credit score so I was not about to let that happen either. In most instances, our credit worthiness exceeds far more than we actually have in the bank. I thought I would throw that one out there, hoping that you'll remember it in the future.

Since I was managing the business with funds I put away for something else, I was later able to hire Carla, a private subcontractor for double duty. Carla was extremely knowledgeable and confident. She was capable of helping with the managerial aspects of the business, as well as performing the duties of lead tutor, which she did with such great finesse. By doing so, I was able to kill two birds with one stone.

Frankly, Carla could have managed her own business. She was on the ball, which was an added bonus. Not only that, but Carla could be trusted. She was also a people person. What more could I have asked for? Although Carla was a godly woman, she didn't take any foolishness off of the kids nor their parents. When they got out of hand, she quickly whipped them back into shape. What a priceless asset she was to the entire organization. A word of wisdom to the business owners who might also be reading this book; if you ever find a "Carla" out there who's willing to work by your side, you had better treat her right. You got the right one baby.

Thankfully, as business picked up, I was then able to hire an additional tutor who taught third grade at the time. Sherry was a whiz at math. She could stand toe to toe with any mathematician in the area and still come out on top. The students loved her ingenious style of teaching. The parents gave her raving reviews as well. I really thought I had it going on when she came aboard. She was certainly a welcomed addition to our team.

As the business grew, we also needed the assistance of an experienced van driver to transport our students. The gentleman who drove the van for us just so happen to be my oldest brother, Randy, who had recently retired from out-of-state and relocated back home. He was a great asset and very eager to assist. All I had to do was to inform Randy of the places where the students were going and in a split second, he would be right there to transport them safely to their various destinations. His services alleviated many of my worries regarding how the students were going to get from place to place when attending field trips. It could have actually been a deal breaker for the business if we had not provided transportation during our one of a kind summer program. Parents depended on that additional perk. Hiring a responsible relative made all the difference in the world. Would I do it again? Of course, I would, if Randy proved to be as dependable as he was the first time around. I'm certain that he would. He was very *good* at what he did.

Although all the key people were in place, it was still difficult to take care of the financial aspects of the business and take care of my own personal needs simultaneously. Since the business had recently opened, it was too soon to draw a salary. I knew from the start it was going to take a good five years or so for that to even happen. This is when I really took note of the fact that my own personal savings had taken a serious hit. It came as a result of not paying close attention to exactly where the money was going so things got out of hand. The business had my undivided attention, which entailed doing everything that I could in order to keep it afloat. Honestly, I don't know of any business owner who would not have done the same thing. The business was an investment into my future.

Though I knew it was bad practice to mix my personal funds with monies from the business, I hoped things would turn around before I was in over my head. What a terrible misconception that was. I should have followed my mind, but I did it anyway without even thinking twice. The next time I will have my ducks in a row so this won't happen to me anymore. My money and finances will be all straightened out and *that* will be one less thing I'll ever have to worry about.

You can bet that after experiencing something like that, I was more than happy to keep my business and personal accounts separate. Still, I was adamant that the services provided to my clients were top notch. Although it took a great sum of money to make something like that happen, I do not regret my decision to use my personal finances for maintaining the business. Thank God, it was a huge success. Lord knows I tried my best.

Consequently, my personal bank account was nowhere near where it should have been as a result. At one point, I recall having only $500 to my name in my checking account. That meant the world to me at the time. Five-hundred dollars seemed like a million to me. Although it wasn't very much I knew I had to "make it stretch." There was no room for pedicures, facial, or waxing in the budget. With that being the case, I scaled back on groceries and laundry items that would ordinarily eat up a good chunk of the money set aside for the month.

I have always shared this little story with women regarding their finances because I wanted to show them the importance of having some money in an account for emergencies. We all know that emergencies seem to pop up out of nowhere when least expected. With $500 on hand, a one-way ticket could be easily purchased to just about any place in the world, regardless of the means of transportation. We never know when we might have to leave town unexpectedly.

Overseeing a small business was a humbling experience, but I managed to figure out why my finances had taken such a hit. My problem was that I constantly pulled money out of my personal accounts to cover some of the business expenditures, thinking that I would replace it before the end of the month. That was mistake number one. In addition to that, every time I turned around, I was loaning money to someone who swore they would pay it back. Mistake number two. Someone always has their hand out, but where it's time to pay up, they are nowhere to be found. I rarely got a return on anything from anyone I loaned money. The loans should have actually been gifts in most cases.

Nevertheless, as owner, it was solely my responsibility to ensure the business ran smoothly, so that my clients would want to return. No clients, no business. No work, no eat. Operating a business of that magnitude took a great sum of money, if it was going to be successful. However, after being scared out of my wits when I discovered how critical my own personal finances had become, it was obvious that I some work to do.

Ladies, here are a few financial tips that helped me get my finances back on track. I know you have probably heard of them before, but for some reason or another have not put them to use. Please feel free to implement these pointers at your discretion. Remember, this is what has worked for me. Your situation may be slightly different from mine.

My advice to you and other women who may be experiencing financial difficulty is that before you explore these strategies, pray and ask the Lord to show you exactly how to go about implementing them. Again, He did it for me. Next, take a good look at your financial portfolio. Yes, everybody has one, whether we know it or not, but just in case it slipped your mind, I will fill you in. Simply put, a financial portfolio is a layout of all the assets you've accumulated over the years, including stocks, bonds, real estate, savings, and investments. Your financial portfolio will tell it all. By carefully examining your assets, you will have a p-r-e-t-t-y good idea of what you're working with. So, let's get down to business.

One of the first things I did when getting my finances back on track was to establish a realistic Monthly Spending Plan or MSP. An MSP is a simple plan designated for keeping track of the money you plan to spend. "Who plans to spend money these days?" you might be saying to yourself. Well, in reality, this is the nice way of saying; "Don't buy anything that's not on the list." I know this sounds contrary to what we've been taught about saving over the years, however if implemented correctly, an MSP will designate exactly how much you can afford to spend on specific line items, relative to your monthly bills or other items of necessity. This is a great plan to have in place. Normally, it is when we don't plan how we are going to spend our money is what gets us into serious financial trouble. Once again, that old saying comes to mind, "If you fail to plan; you plan to fail." This is with everything we do, not just our money.

The MSP helps to ensure that only certain items are targeted for spending. All other items not listed in the monthly MSP are discretionary or optional. I realize that emergencies do come up, but in order to stay on track, simply include a line item specifically for "emergencies only" in your MSP. This way, you will not have to borrow from anyone when an actual emergency occurs. Implementing an MSP was a great way for me to curtail unnecessary, habitual, or spontaneous spending.

Since I do not particularly care for the "B" word or budget, I decided to make life a little more interesting with my finances by carefully mapping out an MSP that was suitable for my needs. This is what I strongly suggest you do. I started by focusing on the monthly recurring bills that automatically had to be paid, no matter what;

which included mortgage, utilities, a car note at the time, and insurances. There was no wiggle room for negotiations there.

Also, since it has worked well for me over the years to classify my tithes (ten percent of *all* my income from any source) as one of those recurring bills, I made sure it was at the top of my list. This is how I honor the Lord through giving. Malachi 3:8 asks us a tough question that holds us accountable for how we spend our money. It says, *"Will a man rob God? Yet ye rob me. But ye say, Wherein have we robbed thee? In tithes and offering"* (NIV). It is imperative that we give the Lord his portion first. There are no ifs, ands, or buts about it. When we do this, everything else seems to fall into place.

By the way, there is also a promise that comes along with that particular scripture when we chose to obey it. It instructs us to, *"Bring all the tithes into the storehouse, that there may be meat in mine house, and prove me now herein, saith the LORD of hosts, if I will not open you the windows of heaven, and pour you out a blessing, that there will not be room enough to receive it,"* (Malachi 3:10 NIV). Those who choose not to obey will miss out on this great promise. How can we afford not to give back a small portion of what He has given to us? I prefer to give the ten percent and keep the other ninety percent to fulfill my financial obligations. Which would you prefer after realizing the benefits?

As a sidebar, let me give you a word of encouragement that has never failed me yet. Whatever you do, please pay your tithes and offering as a recurring monthly bill. When you do, not only will you please the Lord for your allegiance to Him, which is all that really matters, but you'll be blessed as a result of doing it. One more thing, you will never have to worry about *not* paying your tithes because they will automatically be paid for you, even when you are enjoying a well-deserved vacation in a foreign county of your choice.

Okay, back to our spending plan. Once I finished adding my tithes and offering as a line item, I continued mapping out the remainder of my recurring bills, until I completed this portion of the MSP, which wasn't so cumbersome after all. As part of my MSP, I also listed the miscellaneous bills that had to be paid. This way, I did not have to remember them off the top of my head.

I have also found that using a computer program that suits my purpose works wonders and alleviates a great deal of mathematical stress. These days, we can all live without additional stress, as though we don't have enough on our plates already. If you do not feel comfortable using a computerized program, there is always the good old pen and paper technique. We are certainly used to utilizing that one. There is no need to squabble over this, just do whatever floats your boat. After all, the purpose of this strategy is to get *your* finances in order so that *you* will be financially stable in the years to come.

Another commonly used tip that I want to share with you is the idea of tracking the daily expenses you incur. I can see those wheels turning in your head right now as you're thinking how time-consuming all of this must be. You probably have already surmised that this can be a very tedious task. Well, you are absolutely right, but it works. Let me explain the simple idea of tracking to you, although you've probably heard it a thousand times before. It never hurts to hear good news again from a sincere friend.

Tracking your expenses means just that. You have to jot down every single penny you spend and items you purchased. Initially, I tried to avoid writing down every single transaction by keeping the original store receipts in a tiny white envelope, so they would not get misplaced. This worked for a while, but by the end of the month, the receipts had already started fading. I could not make heads or tails out of them. Then, I really became frustrated. Like it or not, I reverted right back to that same old antiquated method of jotting down all the transactions I made from day to day, which forced me to become even more disciplined. I could not afford to spend a penny more than what I allocated for the items in my MSP.

If I just so happen to forget to jot down a small purchase, it would not affect me as much, because I diligently kept track of all the others. Therefore, my numbers would not be that far off. Before the end of the month, I could easily refer back to my tracking system to see what I had already spent on specific items or services. Most times the results would put a smile on my face and reminded me that everything was falling into place.

With this method of keeping up with my expenditures, I was on the right track for being able to pinpoint where I needed to curtail my spending. Now can you see why it was imperative for me to have a check and balance system in place? I am all for the idea of tracking. It has helped me tremendously over the years. This is why I am elated to share with you how it has worked for me when my finances were out of whack. Now I am able to "lay a finger" on exactly where my money goes every single month; right down to the penny. It looks good on paper, and it certainly feels good to know where my money is going. This way, I am in control at all times.

Initiating a tracking system has taken the guesswork out of where my money goes. Tracking has also enabled me to take a quick glance at which categories could stand a little trimming for the time being or maybe even cut out altogether. With such favorable results, I have become very conscientious about tracking my expenses. I am in the "know" of how my funds are being spent. Perhaps, if I did not like what I saw, I had the ability to change it immediately and stop spending in that particular area. This is one of the many advantages of having a tracking system in place. You are in control and there are no surprises.

Prior to implementing a successful tracking system, accurate record keeping of my spending habits was only wishful thinking. That has all changed, I'm proud to say. Today, I still track my daily expenses. This keeps me on top of things.

Now, I can truly say that tracking has been a blessing in disguise, or I woudn't do it otherwise.

While I was frantically working on getting my finances back in tiptop shape, I also started clipping coupons again, watching for weekly sales from the local grocery stores, and printing my favorite coupons from various websites. I was even trying to determine which stores would double their coupon values for even more of a savings to me. You can say that I was really pinching pennies, but that's okay; I was on a mission. However, there was one thing I had to keep in mind about collecting coupons; I only needed the ones I was going to use for sure. Otherwise, it would have been a waste of time and money by redeeming them just for the sake of their dollar value. Many women can get caught up into something like this and wind up actually spending more than planned. We must be strategic when spending. Those carefree days of spending, just because an item is on sale is over.

Since I was on a serious mission to recover the finances I lost, saving for the long haul was definitely something I desired. I was determined to make it work for me. Although this trick of the trade has been frowned upon by many shoppers who hated waiting in line behind "the coupon lady" I was willing to do whatever it took for me to get my finances in order. I remember chuckling to myself once or twice as the thought of using coupons hit me. I used to be one of those shoppers who dreaded standing in line behind "the lady." Since I learned how couponing can be advantageous in any household, those ill-natured feelings have subsided. Guess who's "the lady" with the coupons now?

In addition to clipping coupons, I stopped eating out as often and started preparing freshly cooked meals at home. I used to eat out several times a week, but that had to be cut out as well. Dining out regularly can put a big dent in your finances. Initially, you may not notice how your funds are slowly dwindling away, but by the end of the month, you can definitely see how swiping your debit card adds up. My excuse for dining out regularly as a single woman was that I could bring home a carryout box and eat the leftovers for lunch the next day. Sounds familiar? My intentions were good and the rationale for eating out sounded rather logical, but those expenses still added up rather quickly. Furthermore, I still had to take into account the funds used for tipping the waiter once I sat down to eat. YES, we're supposed to tip the waiter. Rarely does an individual include tipping as a line item in their personal budgets. Come to think of it that is not a bad idea at all. It helps to be creative when trying to save money.

When I realized I was spending more than I intended on eating out, I quickly learned how to prepare my favorite meals at home. Sometimes, I prepared enough for two or three meals to save time and money. What came to mind at the time was the statement my mom repeatedly said to me when I was younger regarding "stretching my money" but in this case, I was stretching my meals. Not only did I save by eating at home, I enjoyed inviting friends over to sample a delicious homemade dish prepared by yours truly.

As you can see, I was serious about the business of socking away some funds for my future. By starting out on a positive note, I was encouraged to stay on track. This was when I started saving all of my loose change in the famous glass jelly jars. Where they are kept still remains a secret, of course. As time passed, I managed to fill up several more large jars of loose change. For years, I was reluctant to spend any change at all. Every time I felt the weightiness of my purse from the coins, I emptied them into a jar or a different type of container. You'll be amazed at how fast loose change adds up over the years. I am proud to say that I still save change today, however, in much larger containers. Get the picture?

When I realized how quickly my spare change added up, I decided to put my own spin on saving even more. When we discover something that works for us, we should capitalize on it. This is what I did. Every two weeks I would pay myself a reasonable amount, after putting my tithes aside first. Doing so made me feel better about paying my other bills on time, although I did not have many to begin with. This was the advantage that I had over others who were drowning in debt.

Out of the funds with which I paid myself, I went to the bank and exchanged some of it for several rolls of quarters. I did this for two reasons; I knew that quarters would add up faster than any other denominations of money and I vowed not to spend any change regardless of the amount for at least a year. Since I planned not to spend the quarters right away, I placed them in the jar towards my savings along with the other change I emptied from my purse, or found lying around the house. Low and behold, the rolls of quarters have truly made a real difference in my savings plan. This might not sound so exciting to you, but the rolls of quarters really revved up my savings just like that.

Another one of my financial tips that I really get a kick out of is the use of my famous and friendly gift cards, *not* credit cards. There is a HUGE difference between the two, you know. I will share with you what I think about the use of credit cards later on in the chapter. My take on them may come as a surprise to you. Here's what I do for my reloadable gift cards to keep my finances in tack. Before I do, please allow me to say that reloadable gift cards are just that; they're reloadable, which means that additional funds can be added at any time. No mind games there, right? A word of caution, be sure to purchase only the gift cards that can be reloaded free of charge. Watch out for the ones that cost to reload and charge a monthly fee. Those are a BIG rip off.

Now, don't go running out and purchase a whole bunch of gift cards just for the sake of having them. You won't benefit from doing that, plus it takes away from the whole notion of saving. Personally, I only have four reloadable gift cards to keep me on top of my financial game. Remember, the objective here is to save; not spend our money frivolously. I am only going to refer to the gift cards that I use regularly by numbers, not names. I don't want to give the impression that I'm endorsing a particular brand of product or service.

Card number one, is used when I want to run out quickly to get something to eat, specifically during those times when I don't have an opportunity to prepare a hot meal at home that day. Some things just can't be prevented sometimes so we have to be flexible, not foolish, when it comes to our spending habits. Foolish minds are a waste of our time. There must be a balance somewhere. Incidentally, I can use this particular gift card for purchasing something healthy for any meal of the day at one of my favorite locations to eat. For breakfast, a turkey burrito with egg white and veggies, and a drink is usually a great choice. For lunch and dinner, I can grab a sub or salad with all the veggies I desire, a cold drink and chips. A cup of vegetable soup is another item I occasionally purchase when I am in the mood for something hot and rather tasty.

This particular gift card can be used all over, so I make a point of reloading it prior to traveling. Usually, I reload the card bi-weekly, free of charge, until it reaches a certain limit which I determine in advance. By doing so, I will always be able to run out and pick up something healthy to eat without having to dip into my regular grocery funds to purchase a meal or two. Besides, the funds are already pre-loaded on the gift card ahead of time. There will be no additional funds coming out of my pocket if I chose to grab a bite to eat when I am on the run.

Card number two, is the reloadable gift card that I use for grocery purchases only. Once I set my grocery limit for the month, I immediately reload the card with that specified amount, which normally ranges from anywhere between $175 and $200 monthly. Since I only have to buy groceries for myself at the moment, I am able to get away with allocating this small amount for my grocery needs. While shopping, I am always reminded, that I only have a specific amount available on the card that has been allocated for spending solely on grocery items. I know that I can't overspend on my grocery budget, which is quite easy to do these days, since the card will only be approved for the actual amount that's available for purchase.

The good thing about this budgetary technique is that I will not have to use any cash for my grocery purchases. If you're not disciplined, you can go over budget when you have cash on hand by picking up items that you don't even need and tossing them into your grocery cart. When you use your gift card for grocery shopping, you tend to ignore the desire to pick up food items because they are on sale. Again, with the use of a gift card, your food bill is paid in advance. All you really have to do is shop. It doesn't get any better than that.

Card number three, has been designated for household purchases that I buy in bulk from a local business retailer that requires its customers to purchase a membership to shop there. To be perfectly honest with you, I really don't understand the rationale behind having to pay to spend our own money anyway, but since this has been the acceptable practice for years, who am I to squawk about it? Nevertheless, I decided to play it smart when I shop there by also loading funds on the card every payday until it reaches the allocated mount. Since we know how quickly buying in bulk can add up, using the gift card associated with this manufacture really helps to stay within my budget.

Unlike the other gift cards, the fourth and final card, is set aside for larger household items and purchases that I refuse to put on my credit cards. By the way, I only have two major credit cards, one for business and travel expenditures and the other for household and car repairs. I despise the idea of having to pay monthly interest on credit cards. This is money wasted. So, whenever I have to swipe, I am usually prepared to pay the bill in full once it arrives in the mail. Now, back to the gift cards, I made it a habit of adding additional funds to this particular card, so that I would be able to make larger purchases that were rather costly without having to "break the bank". By doing so, I did not have to touch my emergency funds at all, at least not in certain instances. Emergency funds are for emergencies only, not our must-haves. To sum it up, out of all the budgetary techniques I used over the years, the gift card money saving method is by far my favorite. It is convenient and practical. Most times, I don't even have to carry around any cash on me, which helps me to feel a lot safer these days.

For years, women have missed out on many opportunities to get our finances in order for several reasons. For one, we do not know what to do with our finances, or the second reason is that we simply may not have any. Whatever the case, I do not want you to be in the same situation that I was in a few years ago that forced me to closely examine my financial future based on past mistakes. In addition, I wanted to share with you how each of these money saving tips have worked for me since I became a serious saver. It is my desire that you put them to work for you as well. You can begin as early as today.

Saving for retirement is a biggie. Next to sustaining your personal relationship with the Lord, saving for the future is one of the most important things that you must do. I can't say enough about that, so now I will focus on the importance of having a Roth IRA to supplement your retirement income. Although there are many of books out there that were written about finances, each time I read one of them, it sheds new light on what I already know. Now, I am sharing this wealth of information with you so that you can sharpen your knowledge about your finances too. Remember, "Knowledge is power."

Many of the daily conversations I am involved in somehow seem to focus on retirement. This is such a critical stage in all of our lives if we don't plan to work forever. Being able to retire is an event that everyone should enjoy after laboring for many years to earn it. Conversely, it should not be a dreaded event that creeps up on us and slaps us in the face, because we aren't prepared for it. Don't let this happen to you. Think about where you really want to be financially in ten years from now and make plans to get there.

Retiring healthy and living a life without the sound of an alarm clock interrupting your beauty rest every morning is certainly something to look forward to; whether you're prepared for retirement or not. If you are not prepared, it can be a nightmare. Trust me on this one; I have heard so many horror stories about retirement and people not having enough money to live on. Don't panic, my sister; I have some more *good* news for you. The continued wealth of information I am going to share is the exact same information I use to govern my savings plan as well. That is how I know it works.

After my father passed away several years ago, I secured an awesome job in another state, a cold one at that. One of the first things I asked about was the benefits that came along with the package. Although I am very proud to say that I am now working towards my second retirement, there was still work to be done to ensure that my financial future would be where I wanted it to be. At this stage of the game, I did not have time for any more unpleasant surprises. Immediately after securing the position, I asked, "Did the organization match my retirement savings percentage?" THAT'S FREE MONEY. When I found out the answer, I wanted to scream, not because they did, but because they didn't. At least I knew exactly what I needed to do from that point on, which was to save, save, save. This is one reason why I continuously tell women about the advantages of having a Roth IRA.

Incidentally, a Roth IRA affords us the ability to save for retirement without being taxed on those funds at a time in our lives when we need every nickel and dime we can get. Of course, there are limitations surrounding the amount of funds that can be deposited into a Roth, but any amount we save is a plus. The funds we deposit into a Roth IRA have been taxed already. Depending on our age, we can deposit a specific amount into a Roth for future use. For example, individuals who are fifty and younger can deposit a maximum of $5500 annually into a Roth. Individuals who are fifty and older can deposit a maximum of $6500 into a Roth account per year, according to numerous financial experts.

I know that might not sound like a lot to you, but if you do the math times ten years or more, that's a good chunk of money, compared to depositing pre-taxed funds into an account that has to be taxed later on. Remember, the monies you deposit into a Roth *must* have already been taxed. That's a good thing. When we need our funds most, usually during our retirement years, we will be able to tap into our Roth accounts without a penalty. The monies we have accumulated over the years can be withdrawn in larger quantities, without any stipulations. There is no piggyback taxing going on there.

A Roth is also an individual savings account that can be used in an emergency, although I am not advocating that. This is why I spoke to you previously about including a line item in your MSP designated for "emergencies" only. Since the monies deposited into a Roth have already been taxed, those funds cannot be taxed again, as previously stated. However, if funds from a Roth must be withdrawn for any reason, there is a catch to it. You will only be taxed on the interest that has accrued. Needless to say I continue to contribute the maximum amount annually. It has definitely helped to increase my savings for retirement or other unexpected situations that may arise. Whatever you do, don't miss out on this extremely important financial tool that can help to get your retirement future into shape.

Having a Roth as an additional stream of income in your retirement years is a great way to put your mind at ease. However, it is certainly not enough. Therefore, my advice to you is that you explore other money saving options that at your fingertips, in order to help you secure the financial future you deserve. These options might include taking a look at TSA's (Tax Shelter Annuity), 401K, or a 403(b). In addition, please examine the advantages of having a Roth 401K and the Traditional IRA (Individual Retirement Account) as possible streams of income. Other investments are also for the taking based on your financial need. I am elated to tell you that it makes a world of difference when you are able to use these tools as vehicles for securing your financial future. They have worked for me. I'm certain they will do justice for you too.

In concluding this chapter, I am honored to see that some of you had the presence of mind not to allow your financial situation to get any worse than it could become. You've taken a stand against what could have potentially destroyed you financially. Yes, we sometimes get into a terrible bind. However, we will no longer need to sit and whine. We vow not to let our struggles turn us around. When it's our time to retire, we *will* be able to settle down. Let's keep a positive attitude about our financial future and I can almost guarantee that our financial future *will* be positive. In the words of Benjamin Franklin, one of the Founding Fathers of the United States, diplomat, and scientist, "An investment in knowledge always pays the best interest."

Exquisite Words of Wisdom

"Money won't create success, the freedom to make it will." Nelson Mandela

Here are ten ways you can ensure a good financial future:

1. *Start by saving early. It gives you more time to save.*
2. *Don't window-shop when you are depressed. Your mind will be all over the place.*
3. *Pay off credit card debt monthly. It saves on the interest.*
4. *Decide whether your desired purchase is a need or a want before spending.*
5. *Relocate to a more affordable city.*
6. *If possible, pay off all debt before retiring.*
7. *Don't hand over your finances to those who can't be trusted. Trust your instincts.*

8. *Keep receipts and return all items purchased out of greed, not need.*
9. *Never allow anyone else to completely control your money.*
10. *Review all accounts and investment documents with your financial advisor regularly.*

~Question of the Day~

Are you financially prepared for the future?

_____

_____

_____

Affirmation: Saving for my future will take precedence over spending to impress those who may not even notice me.

My afterthoughts concerning this affirmation are as follows:

_____

_____

_____

_____

~Goal Setting Exercise ~

My goal for being able to maintain a suitable budget is to

_____

_____

_____

My time-frame to accomplish this goal is

_____

_____

_____

Once I accomplish this goal, I plan to _

_____

_____

_____

~Reflections to Remember~

Now that You Are on Top: What's Next

When you think you have finally arrived, do not forget there were others who were also riding in the same car.

One of the most admirable things we can do for someone else is to help them enjoy the ride to the top while we're on our way.

Being on top does not mean looking down on others. It just means the escalator going down is moving very slowly.

~CHAPTER ELEVEN~

Now that You Are on Top: What's Next

What happens when you think you're "all that"

Everybody is talking about "going for the gusto" these days. Simply put, "going for the gusto" means giving it your best shot when seeking after those things you want out of life. Do we really know what all goes into acquiring some of the things we desire or how would we even act once we have attained them? At the end of the day, we must come to grips with the fact that we didn't get there by ourselves. No one ever does. A word of wisdom to those who may have a chip on their shoulders because they finally made it; there was always someone else holding the rungs of the ladder in case it started to tilt.

On the one hand, we're overjoyed when we've made it to the top, but on the other, we're miserable once we start to drop. We can learn a valuable lesson from those who have "made it" when we discover that it's not at all what it seems. It can be terribly lonely once you've reached the pinnacle of your destination and there is nowhere else to go but down. Unfortunately, this is the way it is for some of us who eagerly climb the ladder of success. How we treat others once we get there will be definitely be a tremendous test.

I know this may sound harsh, but we must do better. Notice I said "we." We're blessed with multiple skills and talents from designing our own line of clothing to developing strategic plans for Fortune 500 businesses, yet we've become complacent. We sit around wasting precious time. More than that we've enrolled in classes or started projects that are just waiting for completion. What's the holdup? Do you realize some folk are paid millions just to think? I bet that would be quite interesting for those who're equipped for that line of work. Who's to say that particular job opportunity would only prosper those who are involved? Not, so. Our talents extend further than we can ever imagine. They're not just for our own well-being. I don't believe in that "I've got mine; you get yours" stuff. We are all in this together when it boils down to survival. The key to *real* success is using our talents unselfishly.

Helping others should be a natural part of every person's responsibility. However, what should come naturally sometimes doesn't. One of the primary reasons we have talents is to help someone else along the way. What good would it do for us to be super talented and incredibly gifted if no one else benefits? Don't you think you would get tired of catering to yourself at some point? There's only so much fixing up we can do before we're completely worn out from doing that alone.

Quite often, I'm reminded of a passage of scripture in Matthew 25:14–30, where it provides us with an inspirational message focusing on "The Parable of the Talents." In the biblical days, parables were short stories with distinctive purposes that served as effectual life lessons for the people to govern themselves by. This compelling story, however, tells us that three servant men were given specific talents according to their abilities to perform them. Incidentally, each of us were given talents. What are you doing with yours? Hopefully, you're putting them to good use.

One of the men was given five talents, which he increased, and I'm sure used to benefit others. The second man was given two talents and did likewise. However, the third man was given only one talent, which he hid. He did not bother doing anything with the talent he was granted. Therefore, sometime later, it was taken from him. The moral of the story is that "if you don't use it, you'll lose it." The trouble is that some of us don't even know how to use what we were given. Instead of hurting others because we don't know how to handle success some of us should learn from our past mistakes by putting our love to the test.

Ladies, please forgive me if I offend you in any way, but someone has to tell you the truth. I don't want this to happen to you. As a matter of fact, it's not even about you. In most instances, we're in an authoritative position where we can easily help others through their crisis. Frankly, the positions we hold doesn't even matter when someone is in need. Who cares what we do for a living when our brother or sister needs help? Unfortunately, I had to learn this the hard way. Now, I'm imparting what I've learned through the years to you so that you can possibly avoid the things I've gone through. No one has to tell me not to hoard what the Lord has given me. After years of wondering around in my wilderness, now, I gladly step up to the plate without any hesitation. The only way to get out of thinking that everything is about us is to show up unexpectedly in someone else's life.

Some of us work tirelessly on our 9 to 5's and when we do finally make it to the top, we forget all about those who helped us to get there. Even I have been guilty of that and had to come down off my "high horse" for a reality check. Believe me, I quickly learned where all of my blessings came from and was eager to share with others where theirs did too. After all I had gone through, there was nothing else for me to lose.

Anyone can easily say, "If it wasn't for this person or that one I wouldn't have made it this far." Well, my dear that may be true, but what happens to you when you finally do arrive to that place called "easy street?" This is the lingo used when pointing out that someone has got it made in the shade. Will you get the "big head" and turn your nose up at those who are less fortunate than you? And, once you get there, do you want everyone to notice *you?*

You and I both know of people who have made it to the top by hook or crook, but once they've gotten there, they've acted as though they didn't even know those of us who helped them to get there in the first place. Oh, how soon do some of us forget? Isn't it funny how this happens? I think it's one of the most hilarious things in the world, besides the fact that those individuals think they don't need any of us once they've become top-notch. Well, I have news for them. The same people they gave the cold shoulder to when they were out on the town with the boss will be the same ones they'll have to face during times of adversity. You just watch and see.

Let me tell you a little secret. Most people who made it to the top will tell you that it can be a very lonely place if no one is there to continue providing those same encouraging words and giving them pats on the back. Once those reassuring gestures are removed from the equation, success looks totally different. Being on top is hard work. It's even more than a notion to remain there, but once again, those who made it didn't get there by themselves. Don't let anyone pull the wool over your eyes.

People need one another in the good times and especially in the not so good ones as well. Hezekiah Walker, musical artist, said it with such great conviction in his gospel hit, *"I Need You to Survive."* If we keep on living, there will be plenty opportunities to prove just how much we need one another. If you don't believe me, try climbing a ladder without it being propped up against something that's supporting it. What do you think is going to happen to you? Good answer; both you and the ladder will come tumbling down. We must treat everybody with dignity and respect no matter the position we hold or the status we have acquired. We can easily live without position or status. On the other hand, it's not that easy to survive without people.

It's so unfortunate that when blessings come our way, somehow we get beside ourselves. We allow pride and self-glorification to take over. Sometimes we can't stand ourselves because we're so puffed up. It doesn't make much sense to get to the top on the prayers, well wishes, and incitement of others, then pretend we don't know those individuals when we see them again on the streets. Proverbs 16:18 warns us that, *"Pride goeth before destruction, and a haughty spirit before a fall"* (NIV). This is exactly what happens when we get "the big head." In other words, we become arrogant, conceited, and vain and for what? Just as we are able to climb the ladder, others are able to do the same with a little help and reassurance. One thing for sure, we should all recognize that our help comes from the Lord. So, we can take a back seat when we think we really have it going on. Honestly, we don't.

Prayerfully, we're not so naive to believe that some of us got to where we are solely by our own ambition or drive. We are not that powerful to begin with. We've made it to where we are because of the goodness of the Lord. In other words, He has given us favor through the assistance of those

He appointed to help us out. I believe there's an angel assigned to us all because Gabriel can't possibly handle all the mess we get ourselves into whenever there's a crisis. Without the Lord's grace and mercy, where would any of us find ourselves in the scheme of things?

My sisters, you are bound to make it to the top if you continue to put your best foot forward and your faith into action, but how will you act once you've "made it" there? Will you reach back and help another sister or brother to accomplish his (or her) dreams? Or, will your nose be high in the sky pretending to be a beauty queen? Some of us have lost valuable relationships when we've accomplished our desired goals, not because we've worked tirelessly to attain them, but because we didn't know how to act once we did. Here's what happens to some of us when we rise to the top; we stop speaking to those who supported us, quit hanging out with those who lent us a helping hand, and even forget about honoring "the man with the perfect plan." When this happens, we're headed for destruction.

It's really sickening when we leave our friends hanging because we think we have it going on. Who are we kidding? If it wasn't in part for them giving us a leg up, we wouldn't have obtained that position or status from the get go. Most likely, we would be in the same rut we were in, before they prayed us through. We need to stop acting like we're brand new. We were just fortunate to have friends who cared enough about us to go the extra mile. We can't even begin to say we made it by ourselves when clearly there was someone else there willing to help.

Keep these words in mind, my sister, so that you won't let pride get in the way, "If you get "the big head" once you reach the top there will surely be those who'll laugh at you when you begin to drop." Remember those who helped you to get to where you are. Don't go around acting stuck up when you're driving your brand new car. Just as you have made it, there are others who will make it too. The difference is that they're depending on the Lord to help them make it though.

Now that *you're* on top; what's next for you? Don't do like so many others did and end up being a fool. Please help another person when they're down and out. When you reach the top my dear; that's what it's all about. Stop pretending you don't need your loved ones standing by your side. Many have dealt with stressful situation and some have even died.

There's a lesson to be learned in everything we do. So, when you reach the top, my dear, can we depend on *you?* Will you reach out and take the hand of someone who's desperately in need? Or, will you go about your own business while seeking fame and greed? As I bring this chapter to close, there is a lot more that could have been said, but on your way to the top my sister, please remember what you've just read. My prayer today is for us to learn what gratitude is all about, so when we finally reach the top, we'll help another sister out.

Exquisite Words of Wisdom

"The more credit you give away, the more will come back to you. The more you help others, the more they will want to help you." Brian Tracy

Here are ten things you can do to help someone else reach the top:

1. Share your success story.
2. Point out the things they are good at doing.
3. Spend time helping them to develop their talents.
4. Invite them to see your place of employment.
5. Send encouraging notes or emails.
6. Help them to get organized.
7. Look over their resume.
8. Prep them for a job interview.
9. Give them a visual of what they are seeking.
10. Introduce them to other successful people.

~Question of the Day~

We should all strive to make it to the top. However, what will you do to help someone else climb the ladder of success while you're trying to get there yourself?

_____

_____

_____

Affirmation: I am determined to help my brother or sister while on my way to the top. I will continue to lend a helping hand and never ever stop.
My afterthoughts concerning this affirmation are as follows:

_____

_____

~Goal Setting Exercise~

My goal for helping someone else to reach the top is

_____

_____

My time-frame to accomplish this goal is

_____

_____

Once I have accomplished this goal, I plan to

_____

_____

~CONCLUSION~

When I began writing, *Living for the Weekend: A Woman's Cry for Hope* I asked the Lord to equip me with the right words to say, the right audience who would receive what I had to say and the wherewithal to say exactly what He wanted me to say. Wouldn't you know He did just that? As I began to tell my story, it was quite evident that I was a vessel being used to give HOPE to the hopeless, bring JOY to the sorrowful, and EMPOWER women to overcome their struggles. But how was I supposed to do all of that without falling flat on my face? After all, I'd suffered so many hardships myself and was just getting back on my own two feet.

Then, it hit me like a ton of bricks, if my assignment was truly to empower women to bounce back from their failures and shortcomings I certainly had to tell them how the Lord helped me to recover from mine. There was no other way around it. The Lord literally healed my broken heart and took away the hopeless mentality that almost tore my life apart. I'm not ashamed to tell my story anymore. As I proceeded to jot down what He wanted me to say, I was careful to impart wisdom without letting my feelings get in the way. A message of HOPE kept coming to my mind as I jotted down the words that gave meaning to every line.

It has truly been a pleasure to have taken this most memorable journey with you. It is my prayer that the personal experiences, scientific research, and words of wisdom I've shared will resonate in the cornerstone of your mind for a lifetime. For those of you who are contemplating throwing in the towel because the wicked "woes of life" have left a bad taste in your mouth, I challenge you to reactivate your faith. Most times, it's the pain and suffering that propels us into our destiny. So, don't stop reaching and certainly don't look back. There is HOPE for you, no matter what it looks like. Just keep on going in the direction of your dreams and you *will* be victorious no matter how dismal it may seem.

Sometimes, we give up right when we're about to cross over to the next level, due to the weightiness of disgust and abomination. Funny, how we always seem to allow our feelings to get in the way when we're on the brink of bursting out from underneath the clutter of despair. But this is neither the time, nor the season to throw up your hands and surrender because you feel defeated. This is the season to think and react differently. If you can grab hold to what I just said, and hold on tight, you can think your way into a new dimension. Now, don't go out searching for something new; everything you need to soar is right there in

~Conclusion~

front of you. You just have to recognize it and put it to work on your behalf.

In closing, thank you for allowing your fingers to do the walking and your heart to do the talking, as we chatted openly, honestly, and intimately about some of the compelling issues we face as women. Isn't it ironic when we're pouring into the lives of others, we're actually ministering to ourselves? That's how the Lord works. He uses our experiences to bless others and we, in return, receive a blessing as well. It has a domino effect on our lives. When we're provided with a resolution for our own problems nothing should stop us from interceding for others. This is what I refer to as throwing them a lifeline of HOPE. With this safety net in place, those we're destined to help will be less likely to drown in despair.

ABOUT THE AUTHOR

Dr. Robin Elliott currently resides in the Washington, DC Metropolitan area. Her careers over twenty-five years have included administration, supervision, and leadership roles, in both private and public school districts, as well as various institutions of higher education. She is presently the CEO of Life Cares Enterprises, a non-profit organization, whose mission is to transform the lives of hurting women all over the world, so that they will no longer be victimized. Instead, they *will* live victoriously, despite the brokenness that once had them bound.

Her call to a nation of women has made a profound impact on the lives of those who were headed for destruction because they failed to recognize their strength in the midst of trouble. A lack of assertiveness will always give the enemy the upper hand, according to Dr. Elliott. As a result, she has dedicated her life to equipping women with the necessary tools for survival. Her exquisite words of wisdom as an electrifying motivational speaker, author, entrepreneur, and a world certified youth, parent and families coach have empowered women to "*creep* past the pain and *leap* into a glorious future."

Dr. Elliott encourages women to step into their destiny expecting to succeed. With the implementation of scientific research and strategies, that teaches women how to use the *power* that lies within them to beat the odds and live, her creative, yet personal delivery style of motivating women has proven to be among the best. Not only does it usher women into the next level, but it also helps to sustain them through their trials and tribulations.

Dr. Elliott can be contacted at drrelliott@yahoo.com for speaking engagements at conferences, national conventions, circle talks, book studies, workshops, or other special events. She will definitely motivate you to "get up and get going." The past *is* your past. The future *is* your future. But what is life *if* you are afraid to live?

NOTES

1. Kirsten Weir, "The Pain of Social Rejection," *Science Watch* 4 April. 2012: 50.

2. Weir, 53.

3. Marina Pearsons and Debra Smouse, "The Breakup Diet: Why Heartbreak Affects Our Appetite," *Your Tango Love Your Best*, 5 July 2015, 7 Sept. 2015 http://www.yourtango.com/breakups-and-divorce.shtml.

4. Shaunti Feldhahn, *The Good News about Marriage* (Colorado:WaterBrook Multnomal, 2014) 93.

CPSIA information can be obtained at www.ICGtesting.com
Printed in the USA
BVOW08s1908171016

465279BV00002B/4/P